Here's your chance
to outguess the pros! MONDAY MORNING QUARTERBACK lets you call the most dramatic plays from NFL and AFL Championship games and from all the Superbowls of the last 10 years. You're given the situation, the important statistics and then you have four choices of strategies.

At the back of the book you'll find out what the professionals did.

So go ahead!
You've always said you could have done it better than they did. Here's your chance to prove it!

MONDAY MORNING QUARTERBACK

by David S. Neft, Roland T. Johnson, Richard M. Cohen
and Jordan A. Deutsch

tempo
books

Grosset & Dunlap
Publishers New York

ISBN: 0-448-12529-3

A Tempo Book Original
Tempo Books is registered in the U.S. Patent Office

Published simultaneously in Canada
Printed in the United States of America

CONTENTS

Foreword

by Jim Campbell
Librarian/Researcher,
Pro Football
Hall of Fame

"Monday Morning Quarterback," "Grandstand Manager," "Armchair Referee"—is there any one of us who at one time or another couldn't be labeled one or all of these. As long as there is more than one way to approach a situation, whether in sports, business, politics, or life in general, there will be second-guessing. This book provides its readers with a unique opportunity, inviting them to second-guess some of the greatest coaches and players in the history of football.

Second-guessing, or Monday morning quarterbacking, is really a pretty easy thing to do. Using hindsight, which is always 20/20, the Monday morning quarterback can see what didn't work, or what did, and then make his guess.

The thing to remember—and this cannot be expressed too strongly—is that the men who made the decisions on the field did not have the advantage of hindsight. They were forced to make the decision immediately, often under intense pressure in crucial moments of some of the most important football games of the last decade.

I first became aware of Monday morning quarterbacking as a youngster growing up in a pleasant little college town in central Pennsylvania in the 1940s. A follower of the local college team could be heard at every game as his team had the ball: "Hit the line." "Why don't they throw the ball?" Sometimes the team's awesome ground attack would stall, and passing became a necessity. The few times the passes were intercepted, this Monday morning quarterback would immediately cry, "Why don't you run the ball? Every time you throw the ball it either gets intercepted or is incomplete."

The authors of this book have done a truly remarkable job of providing the reader with as much information as possible in order for him to "take his turn under center." Even if second-guessing is not your game, there is a boundless amount of information, statistics, facts, figures, and insight contained within these pages.

The nature of the book and its subject matter will out of necessity make it a sensitive subject with some, but the authors have strived to maintain an objective approach and to show compassion for those whose decisions may not have turned out too well.

For every winner, there is a loser. For every guess, there is a second-guess.

1966

NFL CHAMPIONSHIP 1966

DALLAS	**14**	**3**	**3**	**7-27**
GREEN BAY	**14**	**7**	**7**	**6-34**

First Quarter

G.B.	Pitts, 17 yard pass by Starr (Chandler — kick)
G.B.	Grabowski, 18 yard Fumble recovery return (Chandler — kick)
Dall.	Reeves, 3 yard rush, Villanueva (kick)
Dall.	Perkins, 23 yard rush, Villanueva (kick)

Second Quarter

G.B.	Dale, 51 yard pass by Starr (Chandler — kick)
Dall.	Villanueva, 11 yard field goal

Third Quarter

Dall.	Villanueva, 32 yard field goal
G.B.	Dowler, 16 yard pass by Starr (Chandler — kick)

Fourth Quarter

G.B.	McGee, 28 yard pass by Starr (Kick Blocked)
Dall.	Clarke, 68 yard pass by Meredith (Villanueva — kick)

DALL.	TEAM STATISTICS	G.B.
23	First Downs — Total	19
12	First Downs — Rushing	3
10	First Downs — Passing	14
1	First Downs — Penalty	2
4	Punts — Number	4
32.2	Punts — Average Distance	40.0
3	Punt Returns — Number	0
−9	Punt Returns — Yards	0
0	Interception Ret — Number	1
0	Interception Ret — Yards	0
3	Fumbles — Number	1
1	Fumbles — Lost Ball	1
6	Penalties — Number	2
29	Yards Penalized	23
73	Offensive Plays	57
231	Net Yards	367
3.2	Average Gain	6.4
2	Giveaways	1
1	Takeaways	2
−1	Difference	+1

NFL CHAMPIONSHIP 1966

PLAY #1

The way it started out—with two of the quickest back-to-back touchdowns in playoff history—the 1966 NFL championship game looked as if it would be ''laugher'' for Green Bay. The Cowboys, however, matched those two quickies, and it was 14-14 as the first quarter ended. The Packers then moved ahead, but Dallas doggedly refused to roll over; at one point they were only down by one point, 21-20. A turning point, as it later developed, was a Bob Lilly block of a Don Chandler extra-point attempt. The score was 34-20 after that, but more was to happen. That seemingly insignificant block must have meant something to Dallas, because the team reacted like a ''death row'' convict getting the phone call from the governor while the electric chair is being tested.

Don Meredith marshals a Dallas drive, which began at his 29-yard line. It seems stymied as a Dan Reeves fumble loses 10 yards, but Meredith seems to have a hot hand. Granted, the situation is third and 20, and Meredith will certainly have to throw the ball to keep the drive going, but the Packers don't know where, how, or to whom.

Meredith has a choice of many and varied formations, and a fine selection of receivers. Bob Hayes, author Pete Gent and Frank Clarke are wide-men. Pettis Norman is a fine tight end, who can also get yardage on an occasional end around. Don Perkins and Dan Reeves give other opportunities to vary the attack. Meredith would be in a better position if the yardage were a little shorter than the 20 yards required to move the sticks, but he is a mature quarterback who has faced similar situations many times in his career.

CALL YOUR PLAY:

1. Throw long on a deep post pattern to Frank Clarke in the area covered by Tom Brown. He's considered the weak link (but still a pretty strong one) in the Packer secondary.

2. Line up in a spread formation and have Pettis Norman run an end-around to the left side.

3. Have Dan Reeves throw the halfback-option pass down the right sideline to Bob Hayes crossing from the left.

4. Call Perkins on a slant at right tackle, resigning yourself to punting on next down.

NFL CHAMPIONSHIP 1966

PLAY #2

The Dallas defense is as high as their offense. The great Packer line just can't keep the Cowboys off of Bart Starr. Dave Edwards sacks Starr for a loss of 8 yards on first down. Willie Townes deflects Starr's attempted pass on the next play, and on third down Lee Roy Jordan turns a swing pass to Jim Taylor into a 7-yard loss. It's fourth down and 15 to go for the Pack at their 31-yard line. Green Bay has no choice but to kick. Don Chandler, a usually reliable punter and placekicker, picks a bad time to "shank" one. The ball goes out of bounds at the Packers' 47-yard line, when a good punt would probably have given the Cowboys the ball at their 30-yard line or thereabouts.

Dandy Don Meredith wastes no time in moving the Cowboys toward the tying points. A 21-yard pass to Frank Clarke, and an interference call against Tom Brown as he deliberately tangles with Clarke to stop a sure touchdown, give the ball to Dallas with a first down on the Packer 2-yard line with 1:52 left to play.

Can even the Packer defense stop this thrust—four tries at 2 yards? Willie Davis and Ron Kostelnik, Henry Jordan and Lionel Aldridge brace for the charge. Linebackers Ray Nitschke, Dave Robinson, and Lee Roy Caffey are alert. In the secondary, cornerbacks Herb Adderley and Bob Jeter are poised, safeties Willie Wood and Tom Brown await play.

Meredith sends Reeves on an expected pop at the middle—1 yard. Next Meredith rolls out and passes left to Norman. It is dropped, but more importantly, guard Jim Boeke is called for illegal procedure and the ball is moved back to the 6-yard line. The sure touchdown seems even farther away at the moment. Reeves misses a Meredith swing pass. An earlier belt has left him with double vision. Meredith goes at Tom Brown again. He passes to Norman near the goal line, but Brown makes a strong hit and Norman is 2 yards short of victory. Now it all comes down to one play on fourth and 2.

CALL YOUR PLAY:

1. Kick a field goal now and hope somehow to score later.

2. Bring young Walt Garrison in and give him the ball off right tackle.

3. Use Perkins on a draw play. He's not been used this series.

4. Roll out right, keeping or throwing as the defense dictates.

AFL CHAMPIONSHIP 1966

BUFFALO	**7**	**0**	**0**	**0- 7**
KANSAS CITY	**7**	**10**	**0**	**14-31**

First Quarter

K.C.	Arbanas, 29 yard pass from Dawson PAT — Mercer (kick)
BUFF.	Dubenion, 69 yard pass from Kemp PAT — Lusteg (kick)

Second Quarter

K.C.	Taylor, 29 yard pass from Dawson PAT — Mercer (kick)
K.C.	Mercer, 32 yard field goal

Fourth Quarter

K.C.	Garrett, 1 yard rush PAT — Mercer (kick)
K.C.	Garrett, 18 yard rush PAT — Mercer (kick)

TEAM STATISTICS

BUFF.		K.C.
9	First Downs — Total	14
2	First Downs — Rushing	6
7	First Downs — Passing	8
0	First Downs — Penalty	0
8	Punts — Number	6
39.3	Punts — Average Distance	42.3
3	Penalties — Number	4
23	Yards Penalized	40
0	Missed Field Goals	1

AFL CHAMPIONSHIP 1966

PLAY #1

If you've ever been in Buffalo in late December, you know what the weather can be. This January 1st was one of the worst for a championship game. It was cold and wet, and the temperature was soon dipping to the low 30s. The precipitation was rain rather than snow, but it didn't matter. The field was a mess. The Bills' ground crew had used a specially prepared chemical on the field; nevertheless, it was frozen on the sidelines and like a peat bog in the middle. The opening kickoff provided the first break for the Chiefs. It was kind of a "Texas Leaguer," and it was fumbled by Dudley Meredith, a Buffalo defensive tackle and one of the return-wedge blockers, at the Bills' 31-yard line.

Kansas City, under Hank Stram, is noted for several things—the caliber of its talent and the many ways in which Stram and quarterback Lenny Dawson deploy it. During the season, they have been shifting in and out of the "I" formation. On this series they are in a "full-house T."

Dawson has not done much with the Bills' defense on the first two plays of the series, managing only 2 yards, but now on third and 8 from the Bills' 9-yard line, he's got to make a call that will take advantage of this early break. Naturally, a touchdown would be best, but even a field goal will give the advantage to the Chiefs. Will Dawson's call be "for all the marbles"? Or will it be a call that keeps the field goal as a possible follow-up? Kansas City kicking is not yet in the hands of Jan Stenerud and is not that stable a department. Mike Mercer currently holds the job, but earlier in the season Tommy Brooker was used.

CALL YOUR PLAY:

1. Call Curtis McClinton on a draw play, leaving closer field position for a field goal if the first-down yards aren't gotten.

2. Throw deep on a "flag" pattern to tight end Fred Arbanas.

3. Sneak toward the middle of the field.

4. Throw to Arbanas, but on a look-in.

AFL CHAMPIONSHIP 1966

PLAY #2

The Bills got back in the game as Jack Kemp, who had been hampered most of the season with a sore arm, shocked the Chiefs with a bomb. Elbert Dubenion, Kemp's speed-burning wide receiver, sprinted to a 69-yard touchdown. Kemp's pass covered more than half the yardage. "Golden Wheels," as Dubenion was known, did the rest by outrunning Chief defensive backs Willie Mitchell and Bobby Hunt.

Both teams are playing somewhat unorthodox football. They are using formations, "sets," and defenses that have not characterized them during the regular season. Kansas City uses ten or twelve formations on offense. Defensively, they play a "5-3 undershift" more than the standard 4-3. Buffalo is "red-dogging" frequently on defense—something not expected.

Kansas City has gotten another touchdown on another 29-yard touchdown pass—this time to Otis Taylor. Taylor did a lot on his own; he left four Bills strewn in his path as he took Dawson's pass downfield into the end zone. But it looks as if Kemp is about to get the Bills right back into the ball game as the second quarter is ending. The Bills have a first down and goal to go at the Kansas City 10-yard line. Actually, the ball is just inside the 10, so it isn't possible to get a first down without getting a touchdown.

Kemp moved his team mostly by passing to AFL Rookie of the Year, Bobby Burnett, a versatile halfback out of Arkansas. Will Kemp continue to pass on the "blitzing" Chiefs, or will he attempt to get the score by using another method? Little look-in passes are a good way to counteract the blitz. At 6'4" and 255 pounds, Paul Costa is the biggest tight end in captivitiy. Couldn't he turn a look-in into a touchdown?

CALL YOUR PLAY:

1. Throw a down-and-out pattern to Bobby Crocket in the end zone, figuring that Dubenion will be getting all the attention.

2. Call a draw play to Wray Carlton, figuring Kansas City will be looking for the pass.

3. Stay with a safe running play, Burnett off right tackle, and take an eventual field goal, if needed.

4. Spring the Statue of Liberty on them.

Thirty Minutes of Equality

SUPER BOWL I
January 15, 1967, at Los Angeles
(Attendance 61,946)

Who would win pro football's first Super Bowl? Experts predicted that the NFL's Green Bay Packers would not even allow the AFL's Kansas City Chiefs on the scoreboard. But after the Packers scored in the first quarter, the Chiefs came back early in the second quarter to tie the game.

With all expectations of an easy rout laid to rest, the Packers went to work. Mixing passes and running plays, quarterback Bart Starr drove Green Bay deep into Kansas City territory, keying on several weak points he had discovered in the Chiefs' defense. He found that the Packers could run at end Chuck Hurston and tackle Andy Rice and throw against Sherrill Headrick, Fred Williamson, and Willie Mitchell; these men had held up against AFL competition but seemed out of their depth against the Packers. Starr especially enjoyed throwing against Williamson, who had bragged that his hammer tackle, which was really only a forearm smash, would wreak havoc with the Packers. In the second half, Williamson himself would be carried from the field unconscious, the victim of a Green Bay "hammer tackle" of sorts.

Moving quite easily through the Chiefs, the Packers scored their second touchdown on a 14-yard run by Jim Taylor, who simply ran over several Chiefs en route to the end zone. Don Chandler's kick made the score 14-7, but Len Dawson, the Chiefs' quarterback, responded with his own passing attack. A 31-yard field goal cut the score to 14-10 at halftime.

Beginning the second half with high hopes, the Chiefs quickly met with a misfortune that let all the air out of them.

Dawson dropped back to pass but was surrounded by a strong Green Bay pass rush; instead of eating the ball and taking the loss, he heaved the ball downfield. Willie Wood of the Packers picked it off and brought it back all the way to the Kansas City 5-yard line. Elijah Pitts carried it over from there, and the game was never the same. Dawson found it much harder to move the ball, and the Chiefs never again threatened to score. The Packers, meanwhile, took firm control of the game with good blocking and tackling. Max McGee's second touchdown catch of the day built the Packer's lead up to 28-10 after three quarters, and Pitts' second touchdown made it 35-10.

SUPER BOWL I

KANSAS CITY	**0**	**10**	**0**	**0-10**
GREEN BAY	**7**	**7**	**14**	**7-35**

First Quarter
G.B. McGee, 37 yard pass from Starr
PAT — Chandler (kick)

Second Quarter
K.C. McClinton, 17 yard pass from Dawson
PAT — Mercer (kick)
G.B. Taylor, 14 yard rush
PAT — Chandler (kick)
K.C. Mercer, 31 yard field goal

Third Quarter
G.B. Pitts, 5 yard rush
PAT — Chandler (kick)
G.B. McGee, 13 yard pass from Starr
PAT — Chandler (kick)

Fourth Quarter
G.B. Pitts, 1 yard rush
PAT — Chandler (kick)

TEAM STATISTICS

K.C.		G.B.
17	First Downs — Total	21
4	First Downs — Rushing	10
12	First Downs — Passing	11
1	First Downs — Penalty	0
1	Fumbles — Number	1
0	Fumbles — Lost Ball	0
4	Penalties — Number	4
26	Yards Penalized	40
64	Total Offensive Plays	64
239	Total Net Yards	358
3.7	Average Gain	5.6
1	Missed Field Goals	0
1	Giveaways	1
1	Takeaways	1
0	Difference	0

*includes Punts

SUPER BOWL I

PLAY #1

The Packers, after an early exchange with the Chiefs, get possession at their own 20-yard line. Bart Starr is probing the Kansas City defense, which is putting good pressure on the Green Bay signal-caller—especially huge Buck Buchanan, the 6'7", 287-pound defensive tackle. Starr, who calls most of his own plays, now has his club at the 37-yard line of Kansas City, with third and 1. The midway point of the first quarter has passed, but still no score. If the NFL, as is expected, is to show once and for all which is the stronger league, the Packers better make a positive move toward a score.

In pregame media reports, the Pack has made no secret of the fact that they feel Starr's passing game can "pick on" the secondary of the Chiefs, especially the two cornerbacks, Willie Mitchell and Fred "The Hammer" Williamson. One thing to keep in mind is that Starr's most inviting target, 6'5" wide receiver Boyd Dowler, is out of the game at present, and will remain out. Dowler suffered a shoulder separation on the game's sixth play while blocking on a Packer power-sweep. He has been replaced by the seldom used veteran Max McGee.

By this stage in his career, Starr has earned a reputation as a quarterback who will cross up a defense on "third and short" by attempting to throw a deep pass for much more than the needed yardage for a first down. The reasoning behind this is that the team can always gamble on "fourth and short." When Starr has done this, he usually calls a well-thought-out play with a good chance for success, not just a pass thrown up for grabs. Kansas City has to be aware of Starr's tendency. Will they set their defense accordingly? Will Starr chance it now, especially with Dowler out and a rusty McGee in?

CALL YOUR PLAY:

1. Call a play-action pass, first faking the run, and then going deep to McGee on a post pattern in Mitchell's territory.

2. Make the same call, but throw instead to Carroll Dale, the other wide receiver, in Fred Williamson's coverage area.

3. Stick to a "bread and butter" play. Give the ball on a straight handoff to fullback Jim Taylor on a slant over right tackle.

4. Have Starr keep it on quarterback sneak, going on a quick count.

SUPER BOWL I

PLAY #2

Midway into the second quarter of the game, Hank Stram's team is still battling Vince Lombardi's club on an even basis. The score is tied at 7-7 following a Kansas City touchdown—a play-action call by Dawson that found fullback Curtis McClinton wide open on a 7-yard pass. Green Bay is in a situation similar to the one which resulted in their first score. It's third and 1 at their own 36-yard line this time. Remember, it was third and 1 when Starr hit McGee for the initial touchdown.

To open the series, Green Bay has run on first and second downs. Elijah Pitts, who has replaced "Golden Boy" Paul Hornung most of the season, picked up 6 yards, followed by Jimmy Taylor's 3-yard bust. Both plays were aimed at the Chiefs' right defensive side manned by Buchanan, end Chuck Hurston, and linebacker E. J. Holub. Thus far, the Packers have established their running game. Pitts and Taylor are not running at will, but they seem to be able to get what yards they need when they need them. Starr has also loosened the Kansas City defense by passing not only to his wide receivers, but to his running backs and tight ends.

Having been stung earlier, will Kansas City still be susceptible to Starr throwing deep on "third and short"? Having stung Kansas City earlier, will Starr try to do it again? Things to consider: are the Chiefs more susceptible psychologically, having been beaten, or will they be ready? Is Starr going to be bolder now that he's already victimized the Chiefs, or will he be more conservative with his play-calling? Kansas City could give its cause a big lift by being prepared for a "daring" pass, picking it off and running it back. What will be Starr's call? A conservative running play, another "bomb," or still another unorthodox choice from the Green Bay board of strategy?

CALL YOUR PLAY:

1. When you have a good horse, ride it—go again to McGee in Mitchell's area with a medium-distance pass, off of play-action.

2. Call play-action, but this time throw to Carroll Dale on the opposite side of the playing field.

3. Run Elijah Pitts over the Packers' left tackle at Kansas City's weak right side.

4. Call a quarterback sneak on a long count, hoping to draw Kansas City offside.

SUPER BOWL I

PLAY #3

The first half of the first Super Bowl ends with the Chiefs, somewhat surprisingly, showing a slight statistical advantage over the Packers. A lot of their success is due to a well-conceived game plan of play-action passes, called and executed by quarterback Lenny Dawson. Green Bay's defensive co-ordinator, Phil Bengston, must respect the running fake of these plays, and this gives Dawson the added split seconds he needs to connect with his receivers. In fact, the play that set up Kansas City's touchdown was just such a call—Dawson passed 31 yards to Otis Taylor at the Green Bay 7-yard line. On the next play, which got the touchdown, Dawson had both McClinton and Taylor so open in the end zone that he could have tossed to either one.

Dawson is now in this situation: it is early in the third quarter, the score is 14-10 as a result of Mike Mercer's second-period field goal, and the down and distance is third and 5, with the ball at the Kansas City 49-yard line. Even though the score is close, the Packers are beginning to assert themselves. Kansas City, on the other hand, seems to have lost some of its ability to stay up with the Pack.

Dawson is in a crucial situation. If the young Chiefs from the upstart American Football League are to show the "establishment" National Football League that they are on a par, Dawson has to convert this third-down play—and he hasn't been nearly as successful at this as Starr has been—and keep the drive moving. Should he stay with a good thing and again call a relatively safe play-action pass? Or should he take a page from the Bart Starr book of football strategy and spring something unexpected on the Green Bay defenders?

CALL YOUR PLAY:

1. Call play-action to the left and throw a medium-length pass to tight end Fred Arbanas, whose 15-yard average per catch is very respectable.

2. Call a play-action pass to the opposite side to a speedier Otis Taylor.

3. Curtis McClinton, a hulking 234-pound fullback, on draw play is a good possibility for the 5 yards.

4. Throw deep to Otis Taylor near the goal line, hoping to connect and "psych out" Green Bay.

1967

NFL CHAMPIONSHIP 1967

GREEN BAY	**7**	**7**	**0**	**7-21**
DALLAS	**0**	**10**	**0**	**7-17**

First Quarter

G.B.	Dowler, 8 yard pass from Starr PAT — Chandler (kick)

Second Quarter

G.B.	Dowler, 43 yard pass from Starr PAT — Chandler (kick)
Dal.	Andrie, 7 yard fumble return (by Starr) PAT — Villanueva (kick)
Dal.	Villanueva, 21 yard field goal

Fourth Quarter

Dal.	Rentzel, 50 yard pass from Reeves PAT — Villanueva (kick)
G.B.	Starr, 1 yard rush PAT — Chandler (kick)

TEAM STATISTICS

G.B.		DAL.
18	First Downs — Total	11
5	First Downs — Rushing	4
10	First Downs — Passing	6
3	First Downs — Penalty	1
1	Interception Returns — Number	0
15	Interception Returns — Yards	0
3	Fumbles — Number	3
2	Fumbles — Lost Ball	1
2	Penalties — Number	7
10	Yards Penalized	58
2	Giveaways	2
2	Takeaways	2
0	Difference	0

NFL CHAMPIONSHIP 1967

PLAY #1

The thermometer says all that has to be said about conditions for the NFL championship game—13 degrees below zero. Even though it's -13 degrees on both sides of the field, it seems to be bothering the Cowboys more than it does the Packers. Well it may. The Packers are at home. Dallas just isn't used to this kind of weather. On their bench all kinds of things are being done to keep warm. Even on the playing field, the Cowboys are wearing ski masks and similar cold-weather gear when and where they can. Receivers have gloves on, and these are not the golf gloves the Steelers and Raiders will use in their Ice Bowl of a decade later. Pockets of insulated cloth are sewn on the fronts of Dallas jerseys. Packers have also resorted to this tactic.

Meanwhile, Green Bay has jumped out to an early 7-0 lead. This was the result of what was to become to Green Bay almost a cliché—"a long, sustained ball-control drive." Taking sixteen plays (passes and runs), Bart Starr maneuvered the Pack over the frozen and treacherous turf of Lambeau Field on an 82-yard march.

He's guiding the Pack toward another score as action has moved to the second quarter. At the Dallas 43-yard line, the situation is third down and 1 yard to go. Like "love and marriage" and "horse and carriage," Starr and "third and 1" go together. It's become his bench mark to throw long in this situation. But with the field in the condition it's in, will he chance it now? His running game is pretty much a makeshift deal (no Paul Hornung, no Jimmy Taylor), but he should be able to coax a yard out of Donny Anderson, or Travis Williams, or Chuck Mercein. However, what if he does go for it? Will the Cowboys be expecting it, and can they react to it?

CALL YOUR PLAY:

1. Call a quarterback sneak. Starr should be able to get a yard.

2. Fake a run by Ben Wilson on a play-action pass and throw deep to wide receiver Boyd Dowler.

3. Throw a flare pass to Chuck Mercein coming out of the right side of the backfield.

4. Ben Wilson on a slant to the right behind the blocking of guard Jerry Kramer and tackle Forrest Gregg.

NFL CHAMPIONSHIP 1967

PLAY #2

Taking advantage of Packer miscues, Dallas is still very much in the game at the moment. A short punt near the end of the third quarter gives the Cowboys good field position at their own 45-yard line. The first play of the series picks up 5 yards to midfield. Now the Cowboys have a second and 5, and Don Meredith is awaiting the play from the bench. Tom Landry calls all Dallas plays by personal messenger.

In the Dallas backfield with Dandy Don are running backs Don Perkins, perhaps the most underrated man to ever play in the NFL, and Dan Reeves. Reeves is an interesting case-study. He was a quarterback at the University of South Carolina and was overlooked in the NFL and AFL drafts. He wasn't considered a good enough passer to play quarterback, nor enough of a runner to be a halfback. However, Dallas player-personnel director Gil Brandt is fast becoming a genius at picking up unlikely prospects and turning them into very productive players. Reeves not only made the team and is playing, he's playing well. No runner is "setting the woods on fire," but Reeves and Perkins are getting respectable yardage.

Meredith is in an ideal position for experimentation. He's got two downs at the least, and possibly three, to get the needed 5 yards. Will they choose to remain fairly conservative, or will they thumb through the thick Cowboy play-book and come up with a surprise. Remember, head coach Tom Landry calls all the plays. Don Meredith runs them. Will it be a pass, a run, a combination of the two, all of the above, none of the above?

CALL YOUR PLAY:

1. Run Perkins on a slant at the right.

2. Run Reeves on a slant at the left.

3. Have Reeves throw a halfback-option pass to Lance Rentzel down the left sideline.

4. Have Meredith throw deep into the end zone to Bob Hayes on a fly down the right sideline.

NFL CHAMPIONSHIP 1967

PLAY #3

What happens next in this game is something that if it were a movie script would be laughed at, at best or classified as science-fiction at worst. The Dallas defense has taken away much of the Green Bay offense in the second half. On two series, Green Bay has netted 21 yards, 14 of which were a gift from an interference penalty. With about 4½ minutes left in the game, the Packer defense forces Dallas to punt, turning over the ball to the offense at their own 31-yard line. Green

Bay is after an unprecedented third successive NFL championship. This has to give them added incentive, but will it be enough to overcome a Dallas defense that seemingly gets tougher on each offensive series it faces?

Things start out well for the Packers. Cool and calculating Bart Starr has moved Green Bay close. With his wide receivers double covered, he's going to his running backs with his passes. Donny Anderson and Chuck Mercein are getting good yardage as Dallas defensive backs are slipping on the deteriorating surface. Gradually, Starr gets the offense down to the 1-yard line. It's a first down, so he has four shots at Dallas. But time is running out. Twice he gives to Anderson. Twice it's no gain as Anderson slips on the sloppy turf down at the goal line.

Now 20 seconds are left and Starr has taken his last time-out. He confers with Vince Lombardi. Now he's back in the Packer huddle. It's third down, so Starr has two more attempts (possibly), but no time-outs. The play will have to be the right one to fit the circumstances. A completed pass in the end zone means the game. An incomplete pass stops the clock. A running play had better get the touchdown, since the clock would continue to wind down, and there wouldn't be enough time for a second shot. A field goal will tie and send the game into "sudden death."

CALL YOUR PLAY:

1. Earlier in the drive, Green Bay ran a "sucker" play at Bob Lilly. Gale Gillingham pulled out, and Mercein ran where Gillingham was. It got 10 yards. Will it go again?

2. Throw a pass to Mercein swinging to the left. This has also gotten good yardage.

3. Quarterback sneak.

4. Take the best percentage play—a tying field goal and go for an overtime win.

AFL CHAMPIONSHIP 1967

OAKLAND	**3**	**14**	**10**	**13-40**
HOUSTON	**0**	**0**	**0**	**7- 7**

First Quarter

Oak.	Blanda, 37 yard field goal

Second Quarter

Oak.	Dixon, 69 yard rush
	PAT — Blanda (kick)
Oak.	Kocourek, 17 yard pass from Lamonica
	PAT — Blanda (kick)

Third Quarter

Oak.	Lamonica, 1 yard rush
	PAT — Blanda (kick)
Oak.	Blanda, 40 yard field goal

Fourth Quarter

Oak.	Blanda, 42 yard field goal
Hous.	Frazier, 5 yard pass from Beathard
	PAT — Wittenborn (kick)
Oak.	Blanda, 36 yard field goal
Oak.	Miller, 12 yard pass from Lamonica
	PAT — Blanda (kick)

TEAM STATISTICS

OAK.		HOUS.
18	First Downs — Total	11
11	First Downs — Rushing	4
6	First Downs — Passing	6
1	First Downs — Penalty	1
0	Fumbles — Number	4
0	Fumbles — Lost Ball	2
4	Penalties — Number	7
69	Yards Penalized	45
2	Missed Field Goals	0
0	Giveaways	3
3	Takeaways	0
+3	Difference	−3

AFL CHAMPIONSHIP 1967

PLAY #1

In a game that ends 40-7, there may not be an obvious turning point, but as Oakland buried the Oilers, there had to be a time at which the first shovel was turned. Like all games, even "laughers," they start out close. This game was no different. The early sparring found the clubs pretty much on even terms, but Oakland was learning what it could do. Young Daryle Lamonica had just come over from the Buffalo Bills in a trade. He established a good reputation in Buffalo by coming in on occasion to bail out Jack Kemp and the Bills, but this season was the first for him as a starter—he'd acclimated himself well. So well that he was named the AFL's Player of the Year.

The first quarter sees an Oakland drive stall at the Houston 30-yard line. To make the most of it, the Raiders bring George Blanda in to kick a field goal from 37 yards out. He does, and it's 3-0.

Lamonica has now started another drive. Thus far, he's found out that what had previously been an Oiler soft spot is now a strength. Last season the left side of the Oilers' defense was vulnerable—this year it's tough. Pat Holmes, after being seasoned in the Canadian League, is among the league's finer defensive ends. Rookie George Webster, who will eventually be named to the AFL's All-Time Team, adds more strength. Cornerback Miller Farr makes the left side even stronger and deeper, particularly against the passing game. Conversely, the Houston right side is comparatively easy. As the second period begins, Lamonica is at his own 31-yard line. It's second down and 6 yards are needed to move the sticks.

CALL YOUR PLAY:

1. With Gene Upshaw, an emerging star at left guard leading the way, run fullback Hewritt Dixon on a sweep-left at Houston's weak right side.

2. Go at their strength. Run Pete Banaszak, who'll gain 116 yards on 15 carries today, at the Holmes-Webster-Farr flank.

3. Although Lamonica is not particularly hot pasing today (he'll be 10 of 24), loosen the Oiler left side by sending Fred Biletnikoff at Farr.

4. Try Biletnikoff on an end-around.

The Errors of Youth

SUPER BOWL II
January 14, at Miami
(Attendance 75,546)

The Packers might naturally have suffered a mental letdown after their cliff-hanging NFL championship match with the Dallas Cowboys, but the knowledge that this was Vince Lombardi's last game as head coach gave the team all the incentive it needed against the AFL champion Oakland Raiders. In his nine seasons at Green Bay, Lombardi had turned the Packers from chronic losers to perennial champions, and his players were determined that he go out a winner.

The Oakland Raiders, on the other hand, had just won their first AFL crown by severely thrashing the Houston Oilers in the championship game. Like the Kansas City Chiefs last year, the Raiders had several players obviously good enough for any league, but other Oakland players would have to prove themselves against the Packers. They did, but what hurt the Raiders this day were mistakes.

The first quarter went fairly evenly, with the only scoring coming on Don Chandler's 39-yard field goal. Another Chandler three-pointer upped the score to 6-0 in the second quarter, and then the Raiders made their first costly mistake. The Packers had the ball on their own 38-yard line when Bart Starr dropped back to pass. Someone in the Raider secondary missed his assignment and left Boyd Dowler all alone downfield; Starr hit him with a perfect pass, which he carried to the end zone, with the extra point making the score 13-0.

Daryle Lamonica revived his team's failing spirits, however, by driving the Raiders downfield and hitting Bill Miller with a 23-yard touchdown pass. The Oakland defense then stopped the Packer offense, but Rodger Bird, normally a sure-handed punt returner, called for a fair catch and fumbled the ball. The

Packers recovered near mid-field and converted the break into another Chandler field goal and a 16-7 halftime lead.

Using their ball-control offense, the Packers nursed their lead through the second half and built it up to 33-14 on a Donny Anderson touchdown, a Chandler field goal, and Herb Adderley's return of an interception for a touchdown. Lamonica threw another touchdown pass to Miller in the fourth quarter, but that only made the final score a clear-cut 33-14. Vince Lombardi, retiring to the front office, was going out a winner.

SUPER BOWL II

GREEN BAY	**3**	**13**	**10**	**7-33**
OAKLAND	**0**	**7**	**0**	**7-14**

First Quarter

G.B.	Chandler, 39 yard field goal

Second Quarter

G.B.	Chandler, 20 yard field goal
G.B.	Dowler, 62 yard pass from Starr PAT — Chandler (kick)
Oak.	Miller, 23 yard pass from Lamonica PAT — Blanda (kick)
G.B.	Chandler, 43 yard field goal

Third Quarter

G.B.	Anderson, 2 yard rush PAT — Chandler (kick)
G.B.	Chandler, 31 yard field goal

Fourth Quarter

G.B.	Adderley, 60 yard interception return PAT — Chandler (kick)
Oak.	Miller, 23 yard pass from Lamonica PAT — Blanda (kick)

TEAM STATISTICS

G.B.		OAK.
19	First Downs — Total	16
11	First Downs — Rushing	5
7	First Downs — Passing	10
1	First Downs — Penalties	1
0	Fumbles — Number	3
0	Fumbles — Lost Ball	2
1	Penalties — Number	4
12	Yards Penalized	31
69	Total Offensive Plays	57
322	Total Net Yards	293
4.7	Average Gain	5.1
0	Missed Field Goals	1
0	Giveaways	3
3	Takeaways	0
+3	Difference	−3

SUPER BOWL II

PLAY #1

Green Bay kicks off to the Oakland Raiders and gives up absolutely nothing to the American Football League champions on the first series of the game. Fielding Mike Eischeid's punt with no return, Willie Wood turns the ball over to Bart Starr and the Packer offensive platoon. Starr moves them to the Oakland 32-yard line before bogging down and settling for a fourth-down 39-yard field goal by Packer placekicker Don Chandler.

On the next possession Raider quarterback Daryle Lamonica breaks into Green Bay territory, but barely. From the 48-yard line, Eischeid punts out on the Green Bay 3-yard line. Starr, without much flair, but considerable success, drives his offensive charges to the Raider 36-yard line. A conservative Starr makes the give on third and 1 to Donny Anderson, the young bonus-baby runner who has replaced Paul Hornung for good. Anderson is met in the hole by Raider middle linebacker Dan Connors and third and 1 becomes fourth and 1.

On last down with a yard to go, the Packers are still in a position to experiment against the various Raider defensive alignments. The young Oakland defensive unit features "Gentle Ben" Davidson and cat-quick Tom Keating on the right, with Dan Birdwell and Ike Lassiter on the left. As a unit, the Oakland linebackers are the club's defensive strength. They are young, relatively light, very aggressive, and extremely mobile. Connors, Gus Otto, and Bill Laskey (the last two are the outside men) make up the group. They've been stunting, dancing, blitzing, and moving in and out of the line thus far. Starr has combatted this by using an "unrhythmic" cadence, taking away any advantage gained by the different looks of the defense. Does Vince Lombardi, the coaching legend of Green Bay, feel the need to establish NFL supremacy by going for it on fourth and 1 this early in the game?

CALL YOUR PLAY:

1. Take no chances, instruct Chandler to punt out of bounds as close to the goal as he can.

2. Have Chandler zip on his square-toed shoe and try a field goal. It would be from the 43-yard line.

3. Send Ben Wilson, a surprise Super Bowl starter, on the famed Green Bay power-sweep at the Raider right side for the yard.

4. Pass into the middle to tight end Marv Fleming on a look-in pattern.

SUPER BOWL II

PLAY #2

With 11 minutes to go in the first half, the Packers get the ball back on their 38-yard line with a first and 10. Although they have moved well, the Packers still haven't gotten a touchdown on the AFL champs. This is something that must be on Lombardi's mind, as well as Starr's, as the initial play in the series is called.

The devastating big-back running game of Jimmy Taylor's and Paul Hornung's salad days is gone; but the Green Bay club still reflects Lombardi's basic football philosophy, and Ben Wilson, Donny Anderson, Chuck Mercein, and Travis Williams are turning in creditable performances as running backs. Nevertheless, Starr has thrown more during this season than in years past.

Thus far, this game is no exception. The Pack is running, but they are also throwing considerably. Starr has been passing to his wide receivers rather than to his running backs and tight end. This being first down, the Packers are really under no pressure to pull out all the stops, but a volatile coach such as Lombardi must be frustrated by his team's inability to score a touchdown on the newer league's representatives. Although he has told no one officially, there are rumors that this will be "the master's" last game as head coach of the Green Bay Packers. This too must be in Lombardi's mind and somewhat in the minds of the Packer players as they take on the Raiders. Starr has many options, but just what will he choose to go with. Should he pass, and if so, how and to whom? Should he return to the Packer tradition of old and grind out a time-consuming, punishing ground attack? How will he begin the drive?

CALL YOUR PLAY:

1. Try to spring the 9.3 rookie runner, Travis Williams on a power-sweep right, behind the blocking of Kramer and Forrest Gregg.

2. Try a "blitz-krieg" pass deep to Boyd Dowler, intended to go all the way.

3. Use Wilson on a slant at right tackle to begin what is hoped to be a long, sustained touchdown march.

4. Probe the Oakland secondary with a medium post route to Dale.

SUPER BOWL II

PLAY #3

Leading 16-7 in the third quarter, the Packers begin moving again from their own 18-yard line as the midway point in the period is reached. At their own 40-yard line, the offensive unit is in what has become an all too familiar situation. It's third and 1.

Starr, as we know, has taken a chance in similar situations. The logic behind this is: if you score, you've broken their backs; if you don't score, you've still got a chance to pick up the first down on fourth and short yardage. Keep in mind, however, that Starr has done this so often he is dangerously close to falling into a very predictable habit. Any study of a Green Bay tendency chart (a detailed study of what a team has a tendency to do on a given down, with given yardage, at a given position on the field) will show that Starr elects to go for the "bomb" on this type of situation as often as not.

Starr's reputation—at this time he's thought to be the best in the business—is in fact built on his amazing facility to convert on third down, whether it be long, medium, or short yardage. Oakland, with Al Davis's penchant for leaving little to chance, has to be aware of what the Packers could do in circumstances such as these. Will Starr "go to the well once too often?" If so, how and where? Or will he play it close to the jersey? Another thing to keep in mind is that the ancient wonder of Green Bay, 35-year-old Max McGee, now a year older than in Super Bowl I, is in the Packer line-up. Boyd Dowler has been hurt, but unlike last year's game, this is only a temporary thing. Is McGee an advantage as a receiver, or a disadvantage, since recently Starr has worked much more with Dowler?

CALL YOUR PLAY:

1. Cut down on the possibility of ball-handling errors and have Starr run a sneak.

2. Power-sweep left, with Donny Anderson carrying.

3. Throw a swing pass to Travis Williams coming out of the backfield.

4. On a play-action pass, fake the run and throw deep to old Max McGee—as nearly everyone would expect.

1968

NFL CHAMPIONSHIP 1968

CLEVELAND	**0**	**0**	**0**	**0- 0**
BALTIMORE	**0**	**17**	**7**	**10-34**

Second Quarter

Bal.	Michaels, 28 yard field goal
Bal.	Matte, 1 yard rush PAT — Michaels (kick)
Bal.	Matte, 12 yard rush PAT — Michaels (kick)

Third Quarter

Bal.	Matte, 2 yard rush PAT — Michaels (kick)

Fourth Quarter

Bal.	Michaels, 10 yard field goal
Bal.	Brown, 4 yard run PAT — Michaels (kick)

TEAM STATISTICS

CLE.		BAL.
12	First Downs — Total	22
2	First Downs — Rushing	13
8	First Downs — Passing	8
2	First Downs — Penalty	1
2	Fumbles — Number	2
1	Fumbles — Lost Ball	1
7	Penalties — Number	3
54	Yards Penalized	15
2	Missed Field Goals	0
3	Giveaways	2
2	Takeaways	3
−1	Difference	+1

NFL CHAMPIONSHIP 1968

PLAY #1

No team in the National Football League has been as successful in its history as the Cleveland Browns. But what do you say about a team that loses 34-0? "It was close before the opening kickoff." "Their white uniforms really look clean today." "They looked sharp in the pregame drills." Actually, it took a quarter for Baltimore to begin gaining revenge for one of their most humiliating defeats—the 27-0 whitewashing Cleveland hung on them in the 1964 NFL championship game. After a 0-0 first half in that one, Cleveland did everything to the Colts short of dragging them out of Municipal Stadium and dunking them in the icy waters of Lake Erie. Seventeen points in the third quarter and ten in the last shocked the favored Colts that day.

But this is another day. After a missed Don Cockcroft field-goal attempt, the Colts are now moving. Tom Matte, who played his high-school football at Cleveland Shaw, is making steady, if not long gains. Sometimes the Colts will line up in a "power-I" formation, with John Mackey in the up-back position. Mackey is not entirely strange to the backfield. He was a halfback at Syracuse before finding a home at end. Although the Colts used the formation in 1967, the Browns are the first team to get a look at it in 1968. Thus far, it hasn't given the Colts any big gainers, but it is giving the Cleveland defense something to think about. Matte's gains are largely attributable to oustanding line blocking, supplemented by Mackey's handling of the defensive end and fullback Jerry Hill's work on the outside linebacker. He's also getting running room on traps. Quarterback Earl Morrall got the team to the 21-yard line with running plays. With incomplete passes, he's still got them there, and it's fourth and 7. Will the Colts kick, or are they confident enough (even over-confident) to go for it?

CALL YOUR PLAY:

1. Try the 28-yard field goal. Lou Michaels is your kicking specialist.

2. Use the power-I with Mackey up, and throw to him on a slant.

3. Use the power-I and hand off to Mackey.

4. Pass right to Erich Barnes' territory. He's got his hands full trying to stop Willie Richardson.

AFL CHAMPIONSHIP 1968

NEW YORK	**10**	**3**	**7**	**7-27**
OAKLAND	**0**	**10**	**3**	**10-23**

N.Y.	Maynard, 14 yard pass from Namath PAT — J. Turner (kick)
N.Y.	J. Turner, 33 yard field goal

Second Quarter

Oak.	Biletnikoff, 29 yard pass from Lamonica PAT — Blanda (kick)
N.Y.	J. Turner, 36 yard field goal
Oak.	Blanda, 26 yard field goal

Third Quarter

Oak.	Blanda, 9 yard field goal
N.Y.	Lammons, 20 yard pass from Namath PAT — J. Turner (kick)

Fourth Quarter

Oak.	Blanda, 20 yard field goal
Oak.	Banaszak, 4-yard rush PAT — Blanda (kick)
N.Y.	Maynard, 6 yard pass from Namath PAT — J. Turner (kick)

TEAM STATISTICS

N.Y.		OAK.
25	First Downs — Total	18
9	First Downs — Rushing	3
15	First Downs — Passing	14
1	First Downs — Penalty	1
1	Fumbles — Number	2
1	Fumbles — Lost Ball	0
4	Penalties — Number	2
26	Yards Penalized	23
1	Missed Field Goals	1
2	Giveaways	0
0	Takeaways	2
−2	Difference	+2

AFL CHAMPIONSHIP 1968

PLAY #1

Joe Namath is moving the Jets quickly now that his club has fallen behind for the first time in the game. The early 10-0 Jet lead was eroded down to a 13-13 tie, and now the Jets are on the short end of a 23-20 score, thanks to a costly interception by Atkinson ("Broadway Joe" would call his plays all day with Oakland's rookie cornerback, George Atkinson, in mind).

But the man no less an authority than Vince Lombardi called "the most perfect passer in the game" has been eating up yardage in large chunks. Beginning at his own 20-yard line, he first hit wide receiver George Sauer, Jr. for 10. Then he sent Don Maynard right at George Atkinson on a fly pattern. The wiry veteran Maynard proved that over a decade of pro football hadn't robbed him of any of his speed by taking the patented Namath "bomb" at the Raider 12-yard line. He and Atkinson tumbled to the soggy Shea Stadium playing surface, and the ball was spotted at the Raider 6-yard line.

With a first and goal at the 6-yard line, the Jets appear to be in an enviable position. A Jim Turner "9-iron" shot will tie the game, if Namath cannot get the Jets in for a touchdown. Will this influence how Namath calls his plays? He may want to take as much time as possible with the ball since he didn't use much time getting down here. Namath's running game has been very successful too. Many of the runs by burly Matt Snell and elusive Emerson Boozer have been to the left, directed at the right defensive flank of the Raiders. While Namath supplied the lightning, this pair of backs has thundered for well over 100 yards. Will Namath go with thunder or stick with lightning?

CALL YOUR PLAY:

1. Run Snell off left tackle at the right side of Oakland's defense.

2. Run Boozer off left tackle at the right side of Oakland's defense.

3. Bring in Bill Mathis, the sure-handed, good-blocking, old original New York Titan, and pass to him in the right corner of the end zone.

4. Knees and all, have Namath keep on a sneak.

AFL CHAMPIONSHIP 1968

PLAY #2

Despite Joe Namath's heroics, the game is not over. Daryle Lamonica had his offense in gear and moved the Raiders quickly to the Jet 26-yard line. There within reach of a George Blanda field goal (Blanda has already put three kicks through the uprights, although none as far as the 33 yards this would require), Lamonica begins his play selection.

Daryle got the Raiders to the 26-yard line with a first and 10, but three plays have netted the offense nothing. However, time is not yet an overwhelming factor with 5:54 left in the game. True, a field goal will not do anything but make it close, and coach Johnny Rauch has to be aware of just how quickly Namath can get back anything you would get yourself. But it isn't inconceivable that the Raiders would get the ball back with the score 27-26 and enough time to work the ball down for another shot by Blanda at a winning field goal. So, the fourth-and-10 situation isn't that critical.

If the Raiders go for it, they most logically will have to pass. The yardage needed is a long 10, and the running game hasn't been that much of a factor in their offense today. True, Lamonica hasn't used it much. He'll throw 47 times in the game, but Hewritt Dixon, his powerful fullback, is the only one of his running backs having a decent day. Neither Pete Banaszak nor young Charlie Smith has run that often, but when they did, the results weren't much. Passing, Lamonica has been successful in hitting the tricky Fred Biletnikoff for key gains. Will it be a field-goal try or a gamble at the first down? There is a wind factor at Shea. There always is, but this hasn't seemed to hamper Blanda's previous kicks.

CALL YOUR PLAY:

1. Call a sideline to Biletnikoff, who has forced the Jets to remove cornerback Johnny Sample. Sample is now back.

2. Call a draw play to Hewritt Dixon.

3. Kick a field goal—it would be 33 yards—and kickoff onside.

4. Kick the field goal and kickoff deep—there is till time.

AFL CHAMPIONSHIP 1968

PLAY #3

That droning heard throughout the land was a combination of Monday morning quarterbacks and Raiders' faithful expressing themselves with respect to Coach Rauch's decision on fourth and 10. These reactions, in the true nature of quarterbacks who talk their best games on Mondays, always follow an unsuccessful gamble. No coach is ever conceded the title of "genius" if his decision is the right one, only "idiot" if it doesn't work.

Meanwhile, back on the field, instead of over 5 minutes left and 1 point separating the teams, Oakland is 4 points down and is almost certainly forced to try for a touchdown if and when they get the ball back. This is not too bad a position to be in, even if their defense should give up a Jim Turner-Jet field goal. This would make it 30-23, and a touchdown would still allow a tie. "Sudden Death" isn't the best situation in which to find your team, but it beats the alternative. Someone, however, has looking out for Rauch, and the Raiders appear headed for the winning touchdown. They got the ball back without the Jets scoring, and there are more than 2 minutes left to play. A Warren Wells catch of a 37-yard pass, with an additional 12 yards tacked on for "roughing," gives the Raiders a first and 10 at the Jets' 24-yard line.

Wouldn't it have been nice if the score was now 27-26 and a field goal would do the trick? It's not, so Daryle Lamonica has to go to work and get the touchdown for sure this time. What method will he use? Time is not that vital. In fact, it might be wise to use up quite a bit of it to prevent Joe Willie Namath from getting his hands on the ball again. He's already proved that he doesn't need a lot of time to get 6 points in a hurry.

CALL YOUR PLAY:

1. Call a draw play with Hewritt Dixon taking the ball up the middle.

2. Throw a sideline pattern to Fred Biletnikoff, but keep your backs close to block, or to receive in the event it's necessary.

3. A quarterback sneak on a long count, trying to draw the Jets offside.

4. Charlie Smith off right tackle with Hewritt Dixon making the lead block.

The Ironclad Guarantee

SUPER BOWL III
January 12, at Miami
(Attendance 75,377)

When Joe Namath, three days before the game, said, "I think we'll win it; in fact, I'll guarantee it," people snickered. The New York Jets were close to three-touchdown underdogs against the Baltimore Colts, and everyone expected to see the Colts, an establishment NFL team, clobber the long-haired Jets and shut the mouth of their free-spirit quarterback. Coached by Don Shula, the Colts had a feared defense that mixed zone pass coverage and frequent blitzes and a poised offense led by quarterback Earl Morrall, who had substituted spectacularly during the season for the sore-armed Johnny Unitas.

On offense, the Colts did everything in the first half except score. They drove to the New York 20-yard line only to lose the ball on an interception. They recovered a fumble on the New York 12 only to have Lou Michaels miss a close-range field goal. They sprang Tom Matte loose on a 58-yard run only to suffer another interception to kill the drive. The play that typified the Colts' frustration the best came in the second quarter. On a razzle-dazzle play, Earl Morrall handed the ball off, got it back on a lateral, and looked downfield for a receiver. He never noticed Jimmy Orr free in the end zone, so alone that he was jumping up and down and waving his arms to get attention. Morrall instead threw the ball down the middle right into the arms of New York's Jim Hudson.

The Jets, meanwhile, unexpectedly used the off-tackle smash as their main offensive weapon. With Winston Hill leading the way, fullback Matt Snell repeatedly picked up five and six yards through the right side of the Colt line. Whenever the Colts threw their blitz at Namath, he somehow smelled it out and beat it by shooting a quick pass to George Sauer. Mixing his plays well, Namath led the Jets on an 80-yard drive in twelve plays, with Snell carrying the ball into the end zone from the four-yard line. At halftime, the Jets were ahead 7-0.

The script stayed the same in the second half. The Jets ground out the yardage slowly, scoring on three Jim Turner field goals, while Morrall could not get the Colts on the scoreboard. Johnny Unitas, sore arm and all, took over at quarterback in the final period, and although he drove the Colts to a touchdown, it was too little too late. The Jets had won the Super Bowl 16-7; the AFL had finally triumphed.

SUPER BOWL III

NEW YORK JETS	**0**	**7**	**6**	**3-16**
BALTIMORE	**0**	**0**	**0**	**7- 7**

Second Quarter		
N.Y.	Snell, 4 yard rush PAT — Turner (kick)	5:57
Third Quarter		
N.Y.	Turner, 32 yard field goal	4:52
N.Y.	Turner, 30 yard field goal	11:02
Fourth Quarter		
N.Y.	Turner, 9 yard field goal	1:34
Balt.	Hill, 1 yard rush PAT — Michaels (kick)	11:41

TEAM STATISTICS

N.Y.		BALT.
21	First Downs — Total	18
10	First Downs — Rushing	7
10	First Downs — Passing	9
1	First Downs — Penalty	2
1	Fumbles — Number	1
1	Fumbles — Lost Ball	1
5	Penalties — Number	3
28	Yards Penalized	23
74	Total Offensive Plays	64
337	Total Net Yards	324
4.6	Average Gain	5.1
2	Missed Field Goals	2
1	Giveaways	5
5	Takeaways	1
+0	Difference	−0

SUPER BOWL III

PLAY #1

As the overwhelming favorites, the Colts are having trouble putting points on the board. At times, Earl Morrall directs the club masterfully—something he did so well in this season and which won him the NFL Player of the Year award. This is all the more remarkable since Morrall came to the Colts in training camp and became an emergency starter when Johnny Unitas's golden arm developed problems. In this game, however, when it comes time to get points, the Fates and the Jets prevent Colt scores.

A David Lee punt puts the Jets in a hole at their own 4-yard line as the initial period is about to end. On third and 1, Joe Namath hits his wide receiver, George Sauer, Jr. for what appears to be a first down, but Sauer fumbles at the New York 12-yard line and Morrall is presented with another golden chance. Fullback Jerry Hill is dropped 1 yard behind the line on first down, but reliable Tom Matte gets 7 back and Morrall now has a third and 4 at the Jets' 6. Baltimore head coach Don Shula sends in Tom Mitchell to complement All-Pro tight end John Mackey in a twin-tight end short-yardage formation. Mitchell, a product of Bucknell, is considered a rookie in the NFL, but he has logged a year with the Oakland Raiders of the AFL.

The game is scoreless, but the Jets show signs of erupting while the Colts show a propensity for blowing scoring opportunities. It's imperative that Baltimore doesn't come up empty again. With added blocking, will Morrall run, or will he pass? Should caution be uppermost in Colt minds? A fourth-down field goal will still get some points on the board. Morrall and the Colts can choose from more than one play, but if they are going to swamp the Jets, as most pro football followers (Joe Namath a notable exception) think they will, they better do something here and now.

CALL YOUR PLAY:

1. Run Tom Matte on a sweep for the first down.

2. Call a halfback-option pass, with Matte throwing or running as the Jet defensive unit's reaction dictates.

3. Run Jerry Hill on a tackle slant, angling toward the middle of the field with a first down in mind, but also thinking about field position, should a field goal be necessary.

4. Throw a quick look-in pass to Mitchell, figuring the youngster has a better chance of being open than would Mackey, who would attract much more attention.

SUPER BOWL III

PLAY #2

Missed chances are still plaguing Baltimore as they regain possession at the Jets' 42-yard line with only 43 seconds left in the first half. In a game they figured to control from the very beginning (there were those who felt, going into the game, the Colts could name the score), the Colts are down 0-7. "Broadway Joe" continues to exploit the right defensive side of the Colts, especially with Matt Snell running. Morrall, who bears no resemblance to the gridiron's answer to Cinderella, is having his troubles.

There are those who think at this point it would be better to have Unitas, sore arm and all, guiding the Colt offense. While he might not be able to throw the "bomb," Unitas could possibly direct several methodical drives that could get the Baltimore club untracked and on the board. All of this is speculative since Shula is still going with Morrall.

Morrall opens the series by passing. He looks long, but sees no one open and is forced to dump off to Jerry Hill lurking in the flat. Hill is dropped a yard to the good side of the line of scrimmage. Twenty-five seconds still remain, but a look at the sticks shows 9 yards are needed for a first down and 41 yards for a touchdown. There is still time for several plays, especially if the sideline is used fully to preserve the time showing on the clock. Willie Richardson and wily Jimmy Orr have been getting open on occasion, catching some, dropping others, and being missed by Morrall on still others. After a sideline conference with Don Shula, will the Colts go for a couple of quick sideliners and then the home run, or will they "go for broke" on the upcoming play?

CALL YOUR PLAY:

1. Draw play with Hill running, still leaving time to kick a field goal and get back in the game.

2. Throw to Willie Richardson on a 10- to 12-yard square-out pattern at the sideline.

3. Call Matte on the same sweep that netted 58 yards, but no score, earlier.

4. Call the razzle-dazzle "flea-flicker." This play has Morrall giving to Matte, who then begins running right, stopping and throwing back to Morrall, who then looks downfield for Orr or Richardson at or near the goal line.

SUPER BOWL III

PLAY #3

Down 0-7 at halftime, Shula made a decision. He would give the offense one more try to get something going under the direction of Morrall. If it didn't bring positive results, he would then go to "Mr. Quarterback," Johnny Unitas, despite Johnny U's physical condition. Perhaps just his presence would be enough to shake off whatever it was that was dogging the Colts.

A Tom Matte fumble on the first play of the second half aborted Morrall's "last chance." Shula gave him another series, but still the results, or lack of results, were the same. Unitas is now in the game. Like Morrall, Unitas is unable to get points. At times the old magic reappears, but then it disappears at the most frustrating times (from a Baltimore standpoint). But Unitas has guided the Colts on a 15-play, 80-yard drive and the count is now 16-7, Jets. While the points are welcome, the time (over 5 minutes) is costly to the Colt cause. But a quick touchdown and field goal will win it—provided Joe Willie doesn't get something for the Jets.

Time remaining in the game is 3:14 and the Colts must kick off. Is it too early to try an onside kick? If this is to be the strategy, how exactly will it be worked out. There are several ways to effect an onside kick, and a kicker such as the Colts' Lou Michaels is familiar with all of them. Like a pro tennis player or a professional golfer, a pro football placekicker can use spin or "English" to control the flight of a football and also its bounces. Should the Colts decide to kick onside, Michaels will have to decide what kind of kick it will be and pass along the information to the men most likely to be in position to recover it.

CALL YOUR PLAY:

1. Kick off in regular fashions, kicking it as deeply as possible and hope for a break or at least containment on the Jets' offensive series.

2. "Squib-kick" as deep as possible, hoping the unusual spin will make the ball hard to handle.

3. Kick onside, your precise strategy dictated by how the Jets deploy for the kick.

4. Kickoff medium, with a fleet "cover-man" attempting to get the ball somewhere between the Jets' front line and the blocking wedge.

1969

NFL CHAMPIONSHIP 1969

MINNESOTA	**14**	**10**	**3**	**0-27**
CLEVELAND	**0**	**0**	**0**	**7- 7**

First Quarter		
Minn.	Kapp, 7 yard rush PAT — Cox (kick)	3:48
Minn.	Washington, 75 yard pass from Kapp PAT — Cox (kick)	7:07
Second Quarter		
Minn.	Cox, 30 yard field goal	1:07
Minn.	Osborn, 20 yard rush PAT — Cox (kick)	10:15
Third Quarter		
Minn.	Cox, 32 yard goal	11:18
Fourth Quarter		
Cle.	Collins, 3 yard pass from Nelsen PAT — Cockroft (kick)	1:24

TEAM STATISTICS

MINN.		CLE.
18	First Downs — Total	14
13	First Downs — Rushing	4
5	First Downs — Passing	10
0	First Downs — Penalty	0
0	Fumbles — Number	2
0	Fumbles — Lost Ball	1
3	Penalties — Number	1
33	Yards Penalized	5
0	Giveaways	3
3	Takeaways	0
+3	Difference	−3

NFL CHAMPIONSHIP 1969

PLAY #1

Within the frozen, friendly confines of "the Met," the Vikings are playing the kind of game they play best. With the subtlety of a battering ram, Joe Kapp is bludgeoning away at the Browns. It is only 7-0 in the first quarter, but Kapp is doing what he does best. His style will never be made into an instructional film for young, aspiring quarterbacks, but he gets the job done. The first Viking touchdown is an example. In the newspaper it reads: Kapp, 7yd, rush. In actuality it was strictly "basic Kapp." The call was a smash at the middle of the Browns' line by Viking fullback Bill Brown, but he and Kapp got on the wrong side of one another and Kapp and Brown collided. Instead of a fumble resulting, Kapp simply staggered a step or two and battered his way into the end zone.

Now he's got the Vikes with the ball again, but the yardage isn't coming that easily. It's third and 9 at the 25-yard line of the Vikings, but Kapp has been in tougher situations. The call will most likely be a pass, considering the distance needed, but Kapp might just carry the ball himself or do something else equally unorthodox. Should he pass, he's got the targets to complement his style. Bowlegged, barreling Bill Brown is sure-handed coming out of the backfield. Gene Washington, the Big Ten's hurdle champion, presents Kapp with an inviting deep target from one wide-receiver position. John Henderson is young with great potential at the other split spot. John Beasley, an off-season gold prospector, is a reliable, if not spectacular, receiver at tight end. Ahead and in control of a championship game, the tendency would be for a team to play it conservatively. Will the Vikings subscribe to this theory?

CALL YOUR PLAY:

1. Roll out right, with Kapp keeping—no pass intended.

2. Bill Brown on a smash over right tackle, where a young Ron Yary is already gaining recognition as a power blocker.

3. Go deep to Gene Washington, who is most often matched against 34-year-old Erich Barnes.

4. Kapp on a quarterback sneak.

AFL CHAMPIONSHIP 1969

OAKLAND	**7**	**0**	**0**	**0- 7**
KANSAS CITY	**0**	**7**	**7**	**3-17**

First Quarter

Oak.	Smith, 3 yard rush PAT — Blanda (kick)	14:14

Second Quarter

K.C.	Hayes, 1 yard rush PAT — Stenerud (kick)	13:10

Third Quarter

K.C.	Holmes, 5 yard rush PAT — Stenerud (kick)	11:17

Fourth Quarter

K.C.	Stenerud, 22 yard field goal	10:12

TEAM STATISTICS

OAK.		K.C.
18	First Downs — Total	13
6	First Downs — Rushing	5
10	First Downs — Passing	6
2	First Downs — Penalty	2
1	Fumbles — Number	5
0	Fumbles — Lost Ball	4
5	Penalties — Number	5
45	Yards Penalized	43
4	Giveaways	4
4	Takeaways	4
0	Difference	0

AFL CHAMPIONSHIP 1969

PLAY #1

As predicted, the game is a defensive struggle. Both the Chiefs and the Raiders have strong defensive units, but quarterbacking also figures in the strategy of the game. Lenny Dawson of the Chiefs has been bothered by weak knees all season. He has been spelled by back-up Mike Livingston in five games so far. Oakland is more set at quarterback going into the game, but Daryle Lamonica goes out of the game with a hand injury. George Blanda comes in, but his "miracles" are still a season away. With an ineffective Blanda going nowhere and the Chiefs up by 14-7, rookie Raider head coach John Madden goes back to Daryle Lamonica. His passing is still affected by the injury, but somehow he moves the team. They don't call him "The Mad Bomber" for nothing.

Kansas City, however, finds itself with breathing room as Emmitt Thomas picks off a Lamonica pass at the Chiefs' 20-yard line and brings it back to the Raider 18-yard line before being downed. There is 6:50 showing on the clock. Although Kansas City has been in control much of the way, Lamonica's heroic, "guts" performance shows them that they aren't that far removed from a tie. Dawson will have to produce points. Three downs net only 3 yards against the dug-in Raider defense.

Now it's fourth and 7 at the 15-yard line. Jan Stenerud is within easy field-goal range, but with all that time left, will the 3 points mean that much. The Raiders could come back and take away a game in which they have been dominated for much of the time. What will coach Hank Stram and Dawson decide on—a field goal, a pass, a run? If the Oakland defense should halt this Kansas City drive without giving up any points, could the Chiefs hold a fired-up Raiders' offense?

CALL YOUR PLAY:

1. Take the 22-yard field goal and rely on that tough defense.

2. Call a Statue of Liberty with Otis Taylor taking the ball around right end.

3. Look again to Otis Taylor on a sideline pattern in Nemiah Wilson's area, making sure Taylor is deep enough for the first down, at least.

4. Call a draw play with Robert "The Tank" Holmes carrying up the middle.

An Upsetting Farewell

SUPER BOWL IV
January 11, at New Orleans
(Attendance 80,562)

All of the Kansas City Chiefs wore a patch on their jerseys saying "AFL-10." This referred to the ten-year existence of the AFL, which would fade into oblivion after this game and the AFL All-Star Game a week later. As things turned out, the Chiefs took the AFL out in style by handily beating the NFL champion Minnesota Vikings.

It didn't figure. The Vikings had bullied their way through the NFL with a frightening defense, led by the front four of Jim Marshall, Carl Eller, Alan Page, and Gary Larsen and a ball-control attack paced by tough quarterback Joe Kapp. Odds-makers branded the Vikings as two-touchdown favorites to return the Super Bowl title to the NFL after a year in the possession of the AFL New York Jets.

The Chiefs had been to the Super Bowl before, however, and knew how to prepare better for the fanfare. While the Vikings were awed by the hubbub in New Orleans during the week before the game, the Chiefs seriously set about to avenge their loss to Green Bay in Super Bowl I.

The "I" formation that Kansas City used, concealing the position of their backs until the last moment before the play, gave the Minnesota defense some problems right from the start. The Chiefs assigned two men each to block Marshall and Eller, and this move gave the Kansas City backs room to run. Quarterback Len Dawson also found the Viking zone pass coverage less difficult than had been imagined, and he would complete twelve of seventeen passes through the afternoon.

The Kansas City defensive linemen, meanwhile, were putting hot pressure on Joe Kapp, forcing him to hurry his passes. While the defense harassed Kapp in the first period, the Chiefs got close enough to the goal line for Jan Stenerud to boot a 32-yard field goal to put the Chiefs ahead 3-0.

The second quarter went no better for the Viking attack as

the Chiefs scored 13 points to break the game open. Stenerud kicked another field goal. Mike Garrett scored a touchdown after the Vikings had fumbled deep in their own territory, and Stenerud's third field goal made the score 16-0 at halftime.

The Vikings came out for the second half ready to climb back into the game, and Kapp immediately led them on a 69-yard drive that led to the Vikings' first touchdown. But the Vikes could not score again, and Otis Taylor's brilliant 46-yard run with a short pass made the final score only a little worse, 23-7, in favor of the Chiefs and, for the final time, the AFL.

SUPER BOWL IV

KANSAS CITY	**3**	**13**	**7**	**0-23**
MINNESOTA	**0**	**0**	**7**	**0- 7**

First Quarter

K.C.	Stenerud, 48 yard field goal

Second Quarter

K.C.	Stenerud, 32 yard field goal
K.C.	Stenerud, 25 yard field goal
K.C.	Garrett, 5 yard rush PAT — Stenerud (kick)

Third Quarter

Minn.	Osborn, 4 yard rush PAT — Cox (kick)
K.C.	Taylor, 46 yard pass from Dawson PAT — Stenerud (kick)

TEAM STATISTICS

K.C.		MINN.
18	First Downs — Total	13
8	First Downs — Rushing	2
7	First Downs — Passing	10
3	First Downs — Penalty	1
0	Fumbles — Number	3
0	Fumbles — Lost Ball	2
4	Penalties — Number	6
47	Yards Penalized	67
62	Total Offensive Plays	50
273	Total Net Yards	239
4.4	Average Gain	4.8
0	Missed Field Goals	1
1	Giveaways	5
5	Takeaways	1
+4	Difference	−4

SUPER BOWL IV

PLAY #1

In the early going, the Vikings moved to the Kansas City 39-yard line, but on fourth and 10 (a third-and-10 Joe Kapp pass to tight end John Beasley misconnected), the Vikings punted away. Now the shoe is on the other foot. Lenny Dawson has moved the Chiefs from their 17-yard line to the Minnesota 41-yard line. With first and 10 at the 36-yard line, Kansas City looked in good shape, but a Roy Winston "red-dog" nailed Dawson for a 8-yard loss. The following two plays have netted only 3 yards. Thus, it's fourth and 15 at the 41-yard line of the Vikes.

The Chiefs' options are not as limited as it might appear. They have the American Football League's premier punter in Jerrel Wilson, who brings a 45-yard average into the game. In addition to punter Wilson, Kansas City has one of the AFL's top field-goal specialists, Norwegian skier-turned-kicker Jan Stenerud. Stenerud and Wilson give coach Hank Stram the luxury of pro football's strongest, longest, and most consistent kicking game. How will he use it here, or will he use it here? A field goal attempt could have psychological advantages for the underdog Chiefs. A daring fake punt, if successful, could also devastate the Minnesota psyche. Just having Lenny Dawson "air out" his arm with a long pass might provide an edge for later, if not points now. When a team is the decided underdog and its opponents laugh at its strength—remember that the Chiefs finished second to the Raiders in the AFL's western division, though they obviously won the championship game—you have to have some second thoughts. Will "the Mentor," as Stram likes to call himself, pull something from his psychology book or his play-book?

CALL YOUR PLAY:

1. Play the percentages and have Wilson punt away.

2. Try to out-psyche the Vikes and have Stenerud attempt a 48-yard field goal.

3. Have Wilson fake a punt and pass to Ed Podolak for the first down.

4. Have Dawson throw a fake field-goal formation, giving Minnesota something to think about in the future.

SUPER BOWL IV

PLAY #2

About 4 minutes remain in the first period, and Joe Kapp, on the first possession after Stenerud's long-distance field goal, is moving his ball club. Less than a picture quarterback, Kapp is nevertheless an effective field general, as his appearance in the Super Bowl would indicate. Kapp, an All-America selection as a college player at the University of California, chose to play in the Canadian League instead of the Washington Redskins, the NFL team who drafted him in 1959. Kapp's rough-and-ready style made him something of a legend in the CFL, and Vike general manager Jim Finks and coach Bud Grant brought him down to the States to lead the Minnesota offense, to give it some forceful direction. In his third year with the club, that leadership surfaced.

A roughing-the-kicker penalty has given the Vikings another opportunity, and Kapp now has them at midfield. A third and 8 situation results in a 6-yard gain, Kapp passing to John Henderson. But now it's fourth and 2, with half the field in front of him and half behind him.

Kapp, provided he gets permission from Bud Grant, is in an excellent position to play "one-upmanship" with Kansas City. The Chiefs "stack defense" and oddly-spaced front (either Curley Culp or Buck Buchanan line up on Minnesota center Mick Tingelhoff's nose, and neither one is a bargain for the pivot-man) are presently problems. But by burning them from these formations, the Vikings could swing the mental momentum back their way. A 57-yard field goal is most likely not in the repertoire of kicker Fred Cox, but why should Minnesota settle for 3. A first down off the fourth-and-2 situation could eventually be worth 7 points and give the Vikings the upper hand on the scoreboard and on the mental side of things as well.

CALL YOUR PLAY:

1. Don't risk a "backfire," punt away.

2. Give the ball on a handoff to reliable Bill Brown over Ron Yary's block at right tackle.

3. Have Kapp roll out left on a designed "keeper."

4. Allow Cox to try the kick. If unsuccessful, it would be no worse than a punt. (Later Cox will attempt one from 56 yards. This kick would be 57 yards.)

SUPER BOWL IV

PLAY #3

The Viking defense, with the help of a 22-yard hold penalty, stopped Kansas City as the second half opened, and Joe Kapp put together a drive resembling those of earlier in the season. With more guts than grace, Kapp and runners Bill Brown, Oscar Reed, and Dave Osborn get the Vikings' name on the scoreboard with some numbers behind it. Osborn, following Yary, cracked the end zone from 4 yards out, and Cox's kick made the score read: Kansas City 16 and Minnesota 7, with just under 20 minutes of football to be played.

If Kansas City had visions of nursing a lead, this rebirth of the Minnesota offense should have dispelled them. Dawson would have to move the club, sticking to what had been working best in the game up to this point. The Kansas City strategy was to find the "seams" in the Minnesota zone coverages in the secondary. More specifically, Lenny was to throw in front of Viking cornerbacks Earsell Mackbee and Ed Sharockman. This was basically open all day, helped by the fact that Dave Hill and Jim Tyrer (with some double-teaming help) were very effective in neutralizing the pass rush of the Vikings fine pair of defensive ends, Carl Eller and Jim Marshall. "Purple People-Eater" tackles Alan Page and Gary Larsen also haven't been much of a factor in the game thus far. When Dawson hasn't been picking apart the Vikings' zone, running backs like Mike Garrett, Warren McVea, Robert Holmes, and Wendell Hayes have been darting and dodging very effectively. Dawson, with his "I" formation and other varied "sets" is moving the club again. However, at his 37-yard line he's looking at third and seven. The veteran quarterback is known in Kansas City and around the AFL as "Lenny, the Cool." His coolness is being tested here—also Stram's coaching ability. How will the drive be kept alive, if it is?

CALL YOUR PLAY:

1. Pass left—a square-out route—to wide receiver Frank Pitts, who is giving Viking right cornerback Ed Sharockman all he can handle. Make sure the pattern is at least 7 yards deep.

2. Line up in the tight "I" with two tight ends, both of them in close for blocking, and run Frank Pitts (again) on 51 G-O reverse. This play sets Pitts as a wingback left, and he simply takes a handoff from Dawson as he comes back around the right side of the formation. The flow of the play begins left.

3. Call a draw play with power-back Hayes carrying.

4. Throw long to Otis Taylor over left cornerback Mackbee.

1970

NFC PLAYOFF 1970

SAN FRANCISCO	**3**	**0**	**7**	**0-10**
DALLAS	**0**	**3**	**14**	**0-17**

First Quarter	
S.F.	Gossett, 16 yard field goal
Second Quarter	
Dall.	Clark, 21 yard field goal
Third Quarter	
Dall.	Thomas, 13 yard rush PAT — Clark (kick)
Dall.	Garrison, 5 yard pass from Morton PAT — Clark (kick)
S.F.	Witcher, 26 yard pass from Brodie PAT — Gossett (kick)

TEAM STATISTICS

S.F.		**DALL.**
15	First Downs — Total	22
2	First Downs — Rushing	16
12	First Downs — Passing	5
1	First Downs — Penalty	1
1	Fumbles — Number	4
0	Fumbles — Lost Ball	1
5	Penalties — Number	7
51	Yards Penalized	75
1	Missed Field Goals	2
61	Total Offensive Plays	75
307	Net Yards	319
5.0	Average Gain	4.3
2	Giveaways	1
1	Takeaways	2
−1	Difference	+1

NFC PLAYOFF 1970

PLAY #1

It's Dallas 10 and San Francisco 3 in the third quarter, and when facing a passer of the caliber of John Brodie, that is not a lot of insurance. Compounding the Cowboys' worries is the fact that their passer, Craig Morton, is on the way to a 7-for-22 day. His arm is not 100 percent for this game. Dallas has done well in controlling the game by running the ball. Duane Thomas, a rookie who has come on midway in the season, is having the kind of day that wins cars in the right games.

According to the Dallas game plan, sweeps to the left should work. There are reasons for this. John Niland is blocking, and there are few, if any, better pulling-guards in the NFL. Also the San Francisco right flank is young and inexperienced. Defensive end Bill Belk is the senior member in only his third year in the league. Linebacker Skip Vanderbundt is a soph, and Bruce Taylor is just a rookie—but what a rookie.

As the game unfolds, the wisdom of the game plan is evident. Thomas will eventually get 143 yards. Walt Garrison, the real Dallas cowboy, and Claxton Welch will add another 98 yards—most of it Garrison's.

Now the ball rests at the 5-yard line of San Francisco, the result of an interference call on Mel Phillips, who overguarded Bob Hayes. Hayes had little chance at catching the ball without Philips' interference. Morton is faced with a great opportunity for an insurance score. Can he get it in? Or will San Francisco take away his strong plays, knowing that his arm is probably too sore to do any passing? Roger Staubach is available, but he is not the leader of the Cowboys he will be in the future. Should Landry stick with Morton and hope for the best?

CALL YOUR PLAY:

1. Since Morton can't throw, let him run. He's big and he's strong. How about a sneak?

2. Call play-action, with Thomas faking to the left side and Morton pulling out and hitting Garrison curling right, into the end zone.

3. Stay with strength. Run Thomas on the productive sweep-left.

4. Try to baffle the 49er defense with a "wishbone" formation. Have Bob Hayes as the "up-man." Give him a handoff and let him run wide to the left.

AFC PLAYOFF 1970

BALTIMORE	**3**	**7**	**10**	**7-27**
OAKLAND	**0**	**3**	**7**	**7-17**

First Quarter

Balt.	O'Brien, 16 yard field goal

Second Quarter

Balt.	Bulaich, 2 yard rush PAT — O'Brien (kick)
Oak.	Blanda, 48 yard field goal

Third Quarter

Oak.	Biletnikoff, 38 yard pass from Blanda PAT — Blanda (kick)
Balt.	O'Brien, 23 yard field goal
Balt.	Bulaich, 11 yard rush PAT — O'Brien (kick)

Fourth Quarter

Oak.	Wells, 15 yard pass from Blanda PAT — Blanda (kick)
Balt.	Perkins, 68 yard pass from Unitas PAT — O'Brien (kick)

TEAM STATISTICS

BALT.		OAK.
18	First Downs — Total	16
7	First Downs — Rushing	5
11	First Downs — Passing	10
0	First Downs — Penalty	1
0	Fumbles — Number	1
0	Fumbles — Lost Ball	1
2	Penalties — Number	2
10	Yards Penalized	20
2	Missed Field Goals	0
71	Total Offensive Plays	63
363	Net Yards	336
5.1	Average Gain	5.3
0	Giveaways	4
4	Takeaways	0
+4	Difference	−4

AFC PLAYOFF 1970

PLAY #1

Late in the third period, Johnny Unitas is conducting a Colt drive toward a score that would put some distance between the Colts and the pursuing Oakland Raiders. At 13-10, the Baltimore cause can stand some insurance.

Unitas has been working on the Raiders' cornerbacks all day long. Playing the old AFL "bump and run" defense as well as anyone ever played it, the Oakland secondary defenders have caused Unitas concern. With an injury also hampering his throwing, Unitas will end the day with a rather unimpressive 11 completions for 30 attempts, but "Mr. Quarterback" is toughest when the going is toughest. Twice in this current drive he's made the necessary yardage in clutch third-down situations. (Is there a broadcaster or reporter alive who hasn't once stated that "the name of the game is third down"?)

Unitas now has a key first down at the Raider 11-yard line. A field goal won't be much help, so like all real "pros," Unitas is thinking a "quick six." Will he continue to throw? Detroit Lion castoff Tom Nowatske can be effective blocking or running; he's adept at protecting Johnny U in the pocket or could do the lead blocking on a running play. Big rookie runner Norm Bulaich, thought to be a gamble as a number-one draft choice due to a history of injuries as a college player, is contributing greatly to the Colt effort as a freshman. He lends diversification to the Baltimore attack. The question the Raider defense has to ask itself is: how will Unitas attack us? If they know how, will they know where?

CALL YOUR PLAY:

1. Throw a look-in to tight end John Mackey going into the middle.

2. Run a quarterback sneak with Unitas keeping up the middle.

3. Run Bulaich on a slant at left tackle, with Nowatske throwing the lead block.

4. Dust off the old playground special, the Statue ot Liberty, and surprise the Raiders (and millions of others). Have Bulaich come back to the left and take the ball from Unitas's cocked arm.

AFC PLAYOFF 1970

PLAY #2

Baltimore is still trying its best to get away from the Raiders, but despite losing starting quarterback Daryle Lamonica for the second consecutive year in the championship game, the Raiders are "hangin' tough." Lamonica's injury brought on 43-yard-old George Blanda, thought of more as a placekicker than a quarterback at this stage of his career. Blanda will throw almost as many passes in this game as he did in all of the regular season.

With the gap narrowed to 20-17, Blanda has gotten close, but two interceptions have put an end to two drives. Now it is Johnny Unitas who is moving his team. Strategically, it is a series of moves and countermoves. The Colts have gotten good yardage from fullback Norm Bulaich, but it's some previously unseen "sets" that have gotten the best results. Now at their own 32-yard line with a third and 11, Unitas and Colt coach Don McCafferty have thrown a real "gadget" formation at the Raider defense. It features four (count 'em) wide receivers. The regulars, Eddie Hinton and Roy Jefferson, take their familiar places; but foxy Jimmy Orr is at one of the running back positions for Bulaich, and Ray Perkins (playing with a broken toe) is lined up at tight end, with John Mackey out of the formation. The young Raider head coach, John Madden, counters the Colt move by sending in a fifth defensive back, Nemiah Wilson, a light but quick cornerback. Unitas can do a lot from a formation such as this, mostly pass. But what should the Raider defense look for? They wouldn't dare give the ball to Jimmy Orr on a running play, would they? Whatever the call, it shouldn't be too long. Unitas's arm has allegedly lost its "zing." With five defensive backs thinking pass, wouldn't a run cross them up?

CALL YOUR PLAY:

1. A quarterback sneak.

2. Have "tight end" Perkins break away from the line quickly and take a sideline pass past midfield.

3. Have Perkins slant in from tight end.

4. Go to Roy Jefferson on a deep fly pattern down the right sideline.

Follow the Bouncing Ball

SUPER BOWL V
January 17, at Miami
(Attendance 80,055)

The first Super Bowl under the new merger arrangement ended in high drama after being, for most of the afternoon, a comedy of errors.

The strong defenses of both clubs dominated the first-quarter action, although the Cowboys did score on a 14-yard Mike Clark field goal. Another Clark field goal made the score 6-0 in the second quarter when the Colts tied the score on a fluke play. Baltimore quarterback Johnny Unitas threw a long pass down the center of the field to wide receiver Eddie Hinton; the ball bounced off Hinton's hands, back up into the air, grazed the fingertips of Dallas cornerback Mel Renfro, and came right down to the surprised John Mackey. Taking the ball around mid-field, Mackey sprinted the rest of the way to the end zone. The Cowboys blocked the Baltimore extra point.

On the next Baltimore offensive series, a hard tackle by George Andrie forced Unitas to fumble the ball on his own 29-yard line and sent him out of the game with bruised ribs. Cowboys quarterback Craig Morton, operating with a sore arm, then moved his team down to the 7-yard line, from where a short pass to Duane Thomas scored the only Dallas touchdown of the day. Clark's conversion ran the score to 13-6.

The Colts kept up the parade of mistakes when Jim Duncan fumbled the opening kickoff deep in Baltimore territory. The Cowboys then drove from the 31-yard line to the two-yard line on five plays, with Thomas' hard running the key element. With the ball in the shadows of the goal posts, Thomas fumbled the ball, the Colts recovering on the one-foot line.

With the threat erased, the third quarter settled into a pattern of offensive futility, with neither Morton nor Earl Morrall, filling in for the injured Unitas, able to ignite an attack. With eight minutes left, the Cowboys clung to their 13-6 lead.

At that point, however, a Morton pass bounced off the fingers of fullback Walt Garrison into the hands of Colt safety Rick Volk, who returned the ball 17 yards to the Dallas three-yard line. In short order, Tom Nowatske smashed over for the touchdown, and Jim O'Brien added the tying extra point.

Another Morton pass was intercepted with 1:09 left. Mike Curtis stole the pass on the Dallas 41 and returned it to the 28. Two running plays ran the clock down, and then Jim O'Brien, Baltimore's rookie kicker, booted a 32-yard three-pointer to give the Colts an artistically flawed but nonetheless satisfying 16-13 victory.

SUPER BOWL V

BALTIMORE	**0**	**6**	**0**	**10-16**
DALLAS	**3**	**10**	**0**	**0-13**

First Quarter

Dall.	Clark, 14 yard field goal

Second Quarter

Dall.	Clark, 30 yard field goal
Balt.	Mackey, 75 yard pass from Unitas PAT — O'Brien (kick—blocked)
Dall.	Thomas, 7 yard pass from Morton PAT — Clark (kick)

Fourth Quarter

Balt.	Nowatzke, 2 yard rush PAT — O'Brien (kick)
Balt.	O'Brien, 32 yard field goal

TEAM STATISTICS

BALT.		DALLAS
14	First Downs — Total	10
4	First Downs — Rushing	4
6	First Downs — Passing	5
4	First Downs — Penalty	1
5	Fumbles — Number	1
3	Fumbles — Lost Ball	1
4	Penalties — Number	10
31	Yards Penalized	133
1	Missed Field Goals	0
56	Offensive Plays	59
329	Net Yards	215
5.9	Average Gain	3.7
6	Giveaways	4
4	Takeaways	6
−2	Difference	+2

SUPER BOWL V

PLAY #1

All things considered, Super Bowl V is, at this stage, less than an artistic success. There have been fumbles, dropped passes, tipped passes, interceptions, missed PATs etc., etc., etc. Earl Morrall is again in for an injured Johnny Unitas, who left the game early in the second quarter when a George Andrie hit (Dallas right defensive end) reinjured already tender ribs. The score is Dallas 13 and Baltimore 6. Rookie kicker Jim O'Brien missed the try for the extra point after the Colts scored on the controversial 75-yard touchdown play: Johnny Unitas to Eddie Hinton to Mel Renfro to John Mackey, or Johnny Unitas to Hinton to Mackey (depending with which team your allegiances lie).

Morrall has the Baltimore offense poised at the Dallas 2-yard line. Three times he has sent his rookie power-back, Norm Bulaich, into the line. Three times the Cowboys' "flexed" defensive line has stood off the Colt charge and allowed the light and mobile Dallas linebackers to "head 'Big Boo' off at the pass" with no gain. In the "flex" defense one or more of the Dallas linemen will play a yard back from the ball. This is not the normal alignment for a front four, and it is designed to confuse the blocking assignments of the offensive linemen. To some extent the front four of Larry Cole and George Andrie at ends, and Bob Lilly and Jethro Pugh at tackles has done this, especially with regard to the Colt running game. There are just 21 seconds left in the half, so if Baltimore tries for the 2-yard touchdown and fails, the likelihood of the Cowboys coming back to do something is nearly nonexistent. But if the Colts go for it, what will they try? Meanwhile, a successful 9-yard field goal would close the gap to 13-9.

CALL YOUR PLAY:

1. Go to the well once again with Bulaich on a straight smash at Lilly. This would cut down Lilly's pursuit.

2. Give to Bulaich on a draw play—surely after three unsuccessful attempts, the Cowboys would figure a pass as a possibility and have to respect the drop-back fake.

3. Off the double-tight end formation, cross up Dallas by throwing to Mitchell instead of Mackey.

4. Attempt the field goal—it's only 9 yards.

SUPER BOWL V

PLAY #2

A nearly unbelievable series of turnovers, weird plays, and missed opportunities still finds Dallas ahead of Baltimore 13-6. The Cowboys have taken over at their 20-yard line following a real "weirdo" play—Morrall laterals to Sam Havrilak (a utility running back-wide receiver with collegiate experience as a good passing quarterback at Bucknell), who passes to Eddie Hinton, who appears headed for a touchdown but fumbles through the end zone for a Dallas touchback. Just 9 minutes remain in the game.

Dallas's success in the early part of the game was the running of Walt Garrison and Duane Thomas, but during the second half of the contest the Colt defenders, especially the front four of Bubba Smith, Billy Ray Smith, Fred Miller, and Roy Hilton, have virtually shut down the Cowboys' running game. This forces the Cowboy coach, Tom Landry, to send in more and more passing plays. Quarterback Craig Morton, however, is not particularly effective at throwing at this point in the game. He'll complete only 4 out of 10 and suffer 3 interceptions in the second half. Dallas, nevertheless, can't sit on the lead—or can they?—should they? Garrison on first down got 3 yards, but on second and 7, Morton overthrew Duane Thomas coming out of the backfield. It's now third and 7 at the Cowboy's 23-yard line. Dallas has been throwing fairly safe passes to running backs flaring out of the backfield. Should they continue with this, gamble on something more dramatic, or go even more conservatively and try a run, punting on fourth down if necessary. To keep from losing whatever advantage remains, the Dallas club needs a big play—now!

CALL YOUR PLAY:

1. Call a flare pass to Walt Garrison. He's sure-handed, and the rugged fullback can probably run for the needed yardage if the pass doesn't carry him to the first down. Make the call to the left side of the offensive formation.

2. Use Garrison, but only on a draw play instead of the pass.

3. Send Duane Thomas into the line on a straight smash to the Colt right side—blocking provided by Ralph Neely and John Niland.

4. Quick-kick on third down, hoping to catch the Colts with no one in deep safety, allowing for a long roll of the ball.

SUPER BOWL V

PLAY #3

Time is becoming a definite factor now, and with the score still deadlocked at 13-13, "Sudden Death" is a looming possibility. Dallas and Baltimore take turns at futile late-minute drives, and once again it is Dallas ball with 1:52 left.

The Cowboys are ready to move from the Baltimore 48-yard line. The offensive unit starts here as a result of Bob Hayes' fielding of a David Lee punt out of bounds. There is plenty of time for Morton to engineer the offense downfield for a field-goal attempt, if nothing else. But just how will Morton accomplish this? Duane Thomas is fed the ball on first down, but is dropped for a 1-yard loss by one of the most destructive forces in football at the time, defensive end Bubba Smith. On second down, things get worse. Morton is back to pass, but right back there with him is defensive tackle Fred Miller. Miller drops the Dallas quarterback for a loss of 9 valuable yards. To further add to the woes of the Cowboys, holding is detected and now the Dallas club is at their 27-yard line staring at third and an eternity (actually 34 yards for the first).

Morton takes the snap and the third play unfolds. He passes to Reeves. The ball is off Reeves' hands and into those of Colt middle linebacker, Mike Curtis, at the Dallas 41-yard line. Curtis, a fullback at Duke University and in his early years with the Colts, trundles to the Dallas 28-yard line. Making no attempt to stop the clock, Morrall sends Bulaich into the left side two times for 3 yards. Now the clock is stopped with 9 seconds left in the game and the ball at the 25. A 32-yard field goal seems to be the call. But is it really, and if so, how sound is it? The kicker, a rookie, admittedly doesn't like kicking on the Orange Bowl's artificial surface, especially into 10- to 15-mile-per-hour wind with $15,000 per man riding on the boot.

CALL YOUR PLAY:

1. Try the field goal and hope for the best.

2. Try a fake field goal with a pass for a touchdown or a possible closer field goal.

3. Running out the clock with a safe running play, one with a minimum of ball-handling, and play for the win in overtime.

4. Call a quarterback sneak, hoping to make it all the way to the end zone.

1971

NFC PLAYOFF 1971

DALLAS	**0**	**7**	**0**	**7-14**
SAN FRANCISCO	**0**	**0**	**3**	**0- 3**

Second Quarter
Dall. Hill, 1 yard rush
PAT — Clark (kick)

Third Quarter
S.F. Gossett, 28 yard field goal

Fourth Quarter
Dall. D. Thomas, 2 yard rush
PAT — Clark (kick)

TEAM STATISTICS

DALL.		S.F.
16	First Downs — Total	9
9	First Downs — Rushing	2
7	First Downs — Passing	7
0	First Downs — Penalty	0
2	Fumbles — Number	0
1	Fumbles — Lost Ball	0
2	Penalties — Number	1
30	Yards Penalized	12
3	Missed Field Goals	1
3	Total Offensive Plays	47
244	Net Yards	239
3.5	Average Gain	5.1
1	Giveaways	3
3	Takeaways	1
+2	Difference	−2

NFC PLAYOFF 1971

PLAY #1

Most of the early part of the game is devoted to the traditional NFC playoff practice of probing and fencing. Neither Dallas nor San Francisco has moved the ball well, and the fans sitting between the 40-yard lines are the ones seeing the action from closeup. The entire first quarter has been scoreless, and neither team has put any points on the board so far in the second quarter.

John Brodie, who will use only two running backs all day—Ken Willard and Vic Washington—is throwing more than running. The Dallas defense has been very effective. Willard has been practically shut down. He'll end the day netting only 3 yards on 6 carries. All season long, Willard has been the 49ers bread 'n' butter ball carrier—as he has been throughout his career with the club. Vic Washington is a rookie, but not your run-of-the-mill rook. He's come down from the Canadian League with a firmly established reputation as a pretty slippery kind of runner. Washington is taking up some of the slack created by Willard's ineffectiveness, but still the control of the game is in the hands of the respective defense units.

Heading Dallas's "Doomsday" are Bob Lilly, perhaps one of the greatest defensive lineman the NFC has ever seen, Jethro Pugh, Larry Cole, and George Andrie. Backing them are Lee Roy Jordan, Chuck Howley, and Dave Edwards. A tight secondary completes the defensive platoon. San Francisco actually has a front six. Bill Belk, Cedric Hardman, Tommy Hart, Earl Edwards, Stan Hindman, and "Old Leather" Charley Krueger are members of this interchangeable unit. Their backers are Frank Nunley, Skip Vanderbundt, Dave Wilcox, and a strong secondary. Brodie's current drive has been set back by a penalty, making it third and 8 at the 11-yard line. His position is less than enviable.

CALL YOUR PLAY:

1. San Francisco has been a good "screen and draw" team since the days of Hugh McElhenny. This 1971 club is no different. Go with Willard on a draw play.

2. Now is the time to take the wraps off wide receiver Gene Washington. Go to him deep down the left sideline.

3. Try the screen now, save the draw for later.

4. Run Vic Washington on a slant and resign yourself to a punt.

AFC PLAYOFF 1971

MIAMI	**7**	**0**	**7**	**7-21**
BALTIMORE	**0**	**0**	**0**	**0- 0**

First Quarter
Miami — Warfield, 75 yard pass from Griese
PAT — Yepremian (kick)

Third Quarter
Miami — Anderson, 62 yard interception return
PAT — Yepremian (kick)

Fourth Quarter
Miami — Csonka, 5 yard rush
PAT — Yepremian (kick)

TEAM STATISTICS

MIAMI		BALT.
13	First Downs — Total	16
8	First Downs — Rushing	6
4	First Downs — Passing	10
1	First Downs — Penalty	0
0	Fumbles — Number	1
0	Fumbles — Lost Ball	0
1	Penalties — Number	2
12	Yards Penalized	20
0	Missed Field Goals	3
45	Total Offensive Plays	68
286	Net Yards	302
6.4	Average Gain	4.4
1	Giveaways	3
3	Takeaways	1
+2	Difference	−2

AFC PLAYOFF 1971

PLAY #1

On the first offensive series of the game for Miami, there was no hint of what was to come. It was a short, rather conservative drive. Jim Kiick and Larry Csonka ran a little, but after one first down, Larry Seiple came in to punt to Baltimore.

The next time the Dolphins got the ball, the pattern began repeating itself. Kiick got 5 yards on first down. Coaches, at least offensive ones, like to get that much or more on the first play of a series. Defensive coaches like to have their club hold an opponent to under 3 yards on first. The thinking behind the theory is that on second and 5 you can do many more things with the ball. This gives the defense more to think about. If it is second and, say, 7 or 8 yards, the defensive unit knows that you will have to pass on second or third down, or both, and they can adjust the defensive alignment accordingly. By getting a gain of at least 5 yards, you take this advantage away from the defensive platoon.

Miami, normally a ball-control team on offense, has an additional worry today. Baltimore is also ball-control oriented. In fact, Baltimore "ball-controlled" Miami to death in their last regular-season game. With the two "infantries" engaging each other, the "war" shapes up as having the potential of being a fairly dull affair. Will Miami's game plan include specific strategy to counterattack, or will the Dolphins be content to attempt to "out-ball-control" the Colts? The way Miami plays this second-and-5 situation will give a pretty good indication of how they are prepared for the game.

CALL YOUR PLAY:

1. Call Larry Csonka to blast off right tackle.

2. Statue of Liberty play, with Kiick taking the ball out of Griese's arm and going around right end.

3. Fake a pass and give to Csonka on a draw play up the middle.

4. Call a play-action pass, first faking the run to Csonka, then throwing deep to Paul Warfield.

AFC PLAYOFF 1971

PLAY #2

Miami's only score is that 75-yarder to Warfield. Baltimore is doing the best it can to maintain ball control, but they are handicapped in that starting running backs, Tom Matte and Norm Bulaich, are out with injuries. Nevertheless, Don Nottingham and Don McCauley, two Colt youngsters, are doing all a coach has a right to expect from them.

Nottingham is worth mentioning in some detail. He's 5'10", 210 pounds, and a fullback type out of Kent State University. Because of his physique, he's been dubbed "The Human Bowling Ball." Later, H. Cosell will corrupt this to "butter ball." Regardless, Nottingham is doing the job, something he's been doing since coming to the Colt camp as the very last man taken in the previous NFC player draft.

Johnny Unitas has been moving the team well this drive. It began on the Colt 18-yard line with a fair catch of a Larry Seiple punt. Unitas began by giving to Nottingham for good yardage. He then switched off to McCauley, a big back from Duke, and then moved to a passing game. Now he's using Nottingham again. The Colts get a first and 10 at the 17-yard line, and are moving from there. It's McCauley to the 12-yard line, then Nottingham for no gain, then Nottingham for 3.

This make the sticks read fourth and 2, and it's time for a decision. Should Jim O'Brien be brought in for a fied-goal attempt to close the gap, or will the Colts go for the first down, trying for tying touchdown or settling for a shorter field goal if they run out of downs. If they go for it, what will the choice be? Remember, Johnny Unitas is the Colt quarterback, and he "wrote the book" on calls in situations similar to this one.

CALL YOUR PLAY:

1. Go back to Nottingham once again. Run him off right tackle.

2.Hit left tackle with Don McCauley getting the call.

3. Unitas' legs have shown the wear and tear of a decade and a half in the NFL, but surely he could sneak for 2 yards. Call that.

4. Bring the team's biggest running back, Tom Nowatzke, 6'3" and 230 pounds, into the game. Although the element of surprise would be missing, he could almost fall for the 2 needed yards.

Finally Lassoing the Championship

SUPER BOWL VI
January 16, at New Orleans
(Attendance 80,591)

The Cowboys had ended every season since 1966 with a loss in the playoffs, before finally losing last year in the Super Bowl to Baltimore. But now they were hopeful of kicking that habit with a new quarterback in charge of the offense. Since Roger Staubach had replaced Craig Morton as the starting passer halfway through the season, the Cowboys had won seven straight regular-season games and two playoff games. To end the doubts about their ability to win the big games, the Cowboys would have to beat the Miami Dolphins.

The young Dolphins made their first mistake in the opening period when fullback Larry Csonka muffed a handoff from quarterback Bob Griese on the Dallas 48-yard line. After Dallas recovered the fumble, Staubach led the Cowboys deep into Miami territory before settling for a Mike Clark field goal.

Even in the first quarter, Dallas consistently ate up yardage on the ground, with Duane Thomas and Walt Garrison carrying the ball through gaping holes cut open by Cowboy linemen. The Dallas defense, meanwhile, completely shut off the Miami running attack of Csonka and Jim Kiick. The Cowboys also mixed passes into their attack, and a seven-yard touchdown pass from Staubach to Lance Alworth capped a long Dallas drive in the second period. Although the Dolpins scored on a Garo Yepremian field goal, the Cowboys dominated the first half and took a 10-3 lead into the clubhouse at halftime.

After taking the second-half kickoff, the Cowboys ate up five minutes of the clock with a ball-control drive that featured strong running by Duane Thomas. A pitchout to Thomas for three yards scored the touchdown and made the Dallas lead 17-3.

Trailing by two touchdowns after three periods, the Dolpins desperately needed some offensive fireworks in the fourth quarter. Instead, they ran into disaster. With his team finally on the march, Griese lashed a pass at Kiick at mid-field. Cowboy linebacker Chuck Howley had been knocked down when the pass was thrown, but he jumped up and picked it off in front of Kiick. With a convoy of blockers in front of him, Howley chugged downfield with the ball before running out of gas on the Miami 9. Two running plays moved the ball to the 7, and then Staubach hit Mike Ditka in the end zone with a pass to put the game out of reach for the Dolphins. Mike Clark's extra point made the score 24-3, and although the Dolphins launched a drive deep into Dallas territory, a fumble by Griese ended the last Miami scoring threat of the day.

SUPER BOWL VI

DALLAS	**3**	**7**	**7**	**7-24**
MIAMI	**0**	**3**	**0**	**0- 3**

First Quarter
Dall. Clark, 9 yard field goal

Second Quarter
Dall. Alworth, 7 yard pass from Staubach
PAT — Clark (kick)
Miami Yepremian, 31 yard field goal

Third Quarter
Dall. D. Thomas, 3 yard rush
PAT — Clark (kick)

Fourth Quarter
Dall. Ditka, 7 yard pass from Staubach
PAT — Clark (kick)

TEAM STATISTICS

DALLAS		MIAMI
23	First Downs — Total	10
15	First Downs — Rushing	3
8	First Downs — Passing	7
0	First Downs — Penalty	0
1	Fumbles — Number	2
1	Fumbles — Lost Ball	2
3	Penalties — Number	0
15	Yards Penalized	0
0	Missed Field Goals	1
69	Offensive Plays	44
69	Net Yards	185
5.1	Average Gain	4.2
1	Giveaways	3
3	Takeaways	1
+2	Difference	−2

SUPER BOWL VI

PLAY #1

After fencing for much of the opening part of the game, Dallas is driving deep into Miami territory. This year, Navy veteran Roger Staubach is in the driver's seat. The move started when Chuck Howley recovered a rare, but costly, Larry Csonka fumble on the Dallas 48-yard line. Sticking mostly to a ground game, which features the running of Walt Garrison and Duane Thomas, with an occasional "scramble" thrown in by Staubach himself, the Cowboys are very close to the Dolphins' goal line as the end of the first quarter nears. There is no score in the game, but the Cowboys are in excellent position to change that. The question is: how?

After a first and goal at the 7-yard line, the Cowboys now face fourth and goal at the 2-yard line. Thomas and Garrison have each had a shot at the young Miami "No Name" defense, but could only make minor dents in it. On third and goal at the 2, Staubach called a screenpass to the left, aimed at Duane Thomas. Dick Anderson, the young and able Miami safety, knifes through and holds a squirming Thomas to nothing gained.

Thomas has been effective running left behind the blocks of left tackle Tony Liscio and pulling right guard Blaine Nye; Garrison's success has come going right, sprung by Rayfield Wright and the running blocks of left guard John Niland. Staubach's success has been his improvising. Can they come up with a play to net the necessary yardage. Will they even try, or will Tom Landry stay within the conservative guidelines seemingly set down for Super Bowl games and go for the "chip shot" field goal by kicker Mike Clark. It would be an attempt from the 9-yard line, comparable to an extra point.

CALL YOUR PLAY:

1. Call a running play to the left with Walt Garrison carrying.

2. Call a running play to the right with Duane Thomas carrying.

3. Get on the board first with anything that counts—settle for the 9-yard field goal.

4. Have Staubach roll out right and react to the Miami defense—passing a "dink" to a wide receiver (he has Bob Hayes and Lance Alworth to aim at) or taking it in himself for the score.

SUPER BOWL VI

PLAY #2

Late in the first half of the game, Bob Griese and the Dolphins get the ball after a Staubach-to-Alworth 7-yard touchdown pass has made the score Dallas 10 and Miami 0. Griese has not yet attained the stature he will in the near future as one of the very top quarterbacks in all of pro football. Nevertheless, the young ex-Purdue Boilermaker is conducting a masterful example of the "2-minute drill" under game conditions.

Beginning at his own 32-yard line, after a 12-yard return by Mercury Morris of a Clark kickoff, Griese has brought the AFC champions to the Dallas 24-yard line. While Griese is hitting on passes and passing on every down, it should be noted that time is waning, and Dallas is in a defensive alignment that is a little looser than would be normal. Landry's defenders will concede the short passes, but they are protecting deep against the "home run." Up to this point, the Dolphins have mostly been forced out of their game plan. Normally, they would prefer to play a ball-control type of game—running with Csonka and Jim Kiick, eating up yardage and time; but the running game has not been very effective, and Griese is throwing much more than he usually does or would like to. His passing has gotten the Miami club to where they are at the moment, but even if Griese would like to go back to a running game, he can't. There are no time-outs left, and the clock shows just :08 before the field judge's gun will signal the end of the half.

Is there time for another pass? Will Don Shula settle for 3 points—assuming that little Garo Yepremian can connect from 31 yards out? A touchdown would be a very positive way of ending the drive and the first half—going into the locker room down by just 10-7.

CALL YOUR PLAY:

1. With Dallas hanging back, try passing to Paul Warfield on a post, short of the end zone, and hope he can somehow manage to score.

2. Kick the field goal for the relatively sure 3 points.

3. Flood the end zone with all five eligible receivers, throw and hope.

4. Line up in field-goal formation, but sneak blocker Marv Fleming downfield and have ball-holder George Mira pass to him in the end zone.

SUPER BOWL VI

PLAY #3

The more experienced Dallas Cowboys are pretty much overwhelming Miami statistically. In the first half, total-offense figures are 177 yards for Dallas, while Miami has managed to gain only 74 yards. But the game is still only one play away from being tied, provided that one play is a Dolphin touchdown.

As the Cowboys take the second-half kickoff of Garo Yepremian back to their 24-yard line, they are in a position to finally establish themselves as the dominant team in pro football. Having gotten so far so often, only to miss the "brass ring," will Dallas now have their day and silence the growing number of critics who contend that Dallas has the talent, but not the temperament to win?

Again, Duane Thomas and Walt Garrison are supplying the ground force. On occasion, Staubach hits a fresh Calvin Hill with a flare pass. Because of nagging injuries and lack of work, Hill is not at this stage in his career a perennial 1000-yard rusher, but he is still an important cog in the Cowboy attack. The drive progresses downfield with Staubach using a variety of plays—runs, passes, and scrambles. Thomas has just broken off the longest run from scrimmage of the day—a 23-yard rip, off the right side—to give the Cowboys a first and 10 at the Miami 22-yard line. The drive is moving fluidly, but it can't falter if Dallas is to get the "convincer."

What will Staubach get from the bench as his next call? Will Landry, who is sometimes referred to as the NFC's "oldest quarterback," stay conservative, or will he send in a "gadget play?" Like the rest of the Dallas organization, only more so, Landry must be getting tired of Dallas's "choke-up" label and of references to the team as "next year's champions." He and his team are setting up Miami for the "kill." Will they get it?

CALL YOUR PLAY:

1. Bring Hill in to run, something that he has only done 3 times so far. A sweep to the left with power blocking should start the series off well.

2. With wide receiver Bob Hayes (still the "world's fastest human") set wide to the left, bring him back wide around the right side on a flanker reverse.

3. Bang away with Thomas or Garrison.

4. Throw to Hayes in the end zone on a corner route.

1972

NFC PLAYOFF 1972

WASHINGTON	**0**	**10**	**0**	**16-26**
DALLAS	**0**	**3**	**0**	**0- 3**

Second Quarter

Wash.	Knight, 18 yard field goal
Wash.	Taylor, 15 yard pass from Kilmer PAT — Knight (kick)
Dall.	Fritsch, 35 yard field goal

Fourth Quarter

Wash.	Taylor, 45 yard pass from Kilmer PAT — Knight (kick)
Wash.	Knight, 39 yard field goal
Wash.	Knight,46 yard field goal
Wash.	Knight, 45 yard field goal

TEAM STATISTICS

WASH.		DALL.
16	First Downs — Total	8
4	First Downs — Rushing	3
11	First Downs — Passing	3
1	First Downs — Penalty	2
2	Fumbles — Number	1
1	Fumbles — Lost Ball	1
4	Penalties — Number	4
38	Yards Penalized	30
0	Missed Field Goals	1
82	Total Offensive Plays	45
114	Net Yards	164
4.1	Average Gain	3.8
1	Giveaways	1
1	Takeaways	1
0	Difference	0

NFC PLAYOFF 1972

PLAY #1

"Cowboys and Indians" is a game nearly every kid in the country has played. In the NFC it's still being played—the Washington Redskins and the Dallas Cowboys. Unlike movies, books, television, and neighborhood games, the red men are winning this one. It's well into the second quarter, and the Redskins are up by 3-0 on an 18-yard field goal by Curt Knight, who is kicking with unreal accuracy in the playoffs.

The Cowboys, starting first-round-playoff hero-of-the-game Roger Staubach in place of season-long starter Craig Morton, haven't been able to do much. Neither the running of Calvin Hill and Walt Garrison, nor the passing of Staubach is getting the club anywhere to speak of.

Washington is dominating the play but experiencing some frustration since they are not getting the points to go with the yards. Billy Kilmer, the Redskins' super-gutsy quarterback, is in a third and 10 predicament at his own 28-yard line. On second down he threw incomplete to his outstanding wide receiver Charley Taylor on a sideline pass. Kilmer had hoped to victimize the young Dallas left cornerback, Charlie Waters. Actually, Waters is a safety and a good one, but he had to fill in at cornerback for Herb Adderley, whose age very suddenly caught up with him one afternoon against the New York Giants. Thus far, going at Waters hasn't garnered any points for the Skins.

What will Kilmer do here? He could go long. He could go short. He could run. But logic dictates a pass, if the drive is to be kept alive. Will coach George Allen and Kilmer settle on a logical call? Kilmer will make the final decision, since he calls virtually all of his own plays. Another note: Chuck Howley, the veteran Dallas linebacker who does so much so well, is out of the game. D. D. Lewis, a prospect with much potential but little playing experience, is in his place at right linebacker.

CALL YOUR PLAY:

1. Look for tight end Jerry Smith, who's been ignored so far, on a curl-in pattern run deep enough for the first down.

2. Call a draw play with Larry Brown getting the ball.

3. Call Larry Brown on an end sweep to the right side.

4. Run Taylor on another sideline at Waters, but have him turn it into a "down and out and up," faking a basic sideline route and then turning upfield and going long to take a Kilmer pass.

AFC PLAYOFF 1972

PITTSBURGH	**7**	**0**	**3**	**7-17**
MIAMI	**0**	**7**	**7**	**7-21**

First Quarter

Pitt.	Mullins, Recovery of Pitt fumble in end zone PAT — Gerela (kick)

Second Quarter

Miami	Csonka, 9 yard pass from Morrall PAT — Yepremian (kick)

Third Quarter

Pitt.	Gerela, 14 yard field goal
Miami	Kiick, 2 yard rush PAT — Yepremian (kick)

Fourth Quarter

Miami	Kiick, 3 yard rush PAT — Yepremian (kick)
Pitt.	Young, 12 yard pass from Bradshaw PAT — Gerela (kick)

TEAM STATISTICS

PITT.		MIAMI
13	First Downs — Total	19
6	First Downs — Rushing	11
6	First Downs — Passing	6
1	First Downs — Penalty	2
2	Fumbles — Number	0
0	Fumbles — Lost Ball	0
4	Penalties — Number	2
30	Yards Penalized	19
1	Missed Field Goals	0
48	Total Offensive Plays	65
250	Net Yards	314
5.2	Average Gain	4.8
2	Giveaways	1
1	Takeaways	2
−1	Difference	+1

AFC PLAYOFF 1972

PLAY #1

For Mercury Morris, it's homecoming day. He played his high-school ball in the Pittsburgh district before matriculating to West Texas State. For the rest of the Dolphins and Steelers, it's the AFC championship game. The stands on this unseasonably warm 63-degree day are filled with Steeler faithful, who, after last week's "Immaculate Reception" win over the Oakland Raiders, expect to see their team in Super Bowl VII.

Miami hasn't been able to move much early in the first quarter. Earl Morrall is either passing or running Larry Csonka on every play. Glen Edwards intercepts a Morrall pass intended for Howard Twilley and this leads to an 11-play Steeler touchdown drive.

The rest of the quarter is even, but as it winds down, the Dolphins are driving. Morrall is now using Morris to loosen the Steelers' defense. Occasionally he will throw to Marv Fleming or give to Jim Kiick, as Don Shula rotates Csonka's backfield partners. Near midfield the drive bogs down, and it looks like the Steeler defense is capable of not only putting the damper on Miami's hopes for a return engagement in the Super Bowl, but ending their winning streak at 15. It's fourth and 5 at midfield.

During pregame practice, Garo Yepremian was getting good distance and height on his field-goal tries. In order to shake up his troops and negate the advantage generated by the enthusiastic Steeler fans, will Shula allow a long-distance field-goal attempt. A punt seems the only logical call, but Shula's sideline expression clearly shows he's irritated about the ineffectiveness of the Dolphins' play. Would this be the spot to gamble? Pittsburgh's offense isn't that devastating yet, and there is nothing wrong with the way Miami's defense is playing, should they be called on to rescue the club from a gamble that backfires.

CALL YOUR PLAY:

1. Fake a punt and have Larry Seiple run from punt formation.

2. Punt, angling the ball out of bounds as deeply as possible, without, of course, going into the end zone for a touchback.

3. Try the coast-to-coast field goal.

4. Throw a pass from punt formation to one of the punt-coverage men. Jim Mandich is in on this team. He's got good hands.

AFC PLAYOFF 1972

PLAY #2

The score at halftime is 7-7. Now, as the third quarter begins, the game is obviously not going as expected. A "disoriented" Terry Bradshaw (Steeler trainer Ralph Berlin supplied the quote) has been replaced by Terry Hanratty. Shula, still looking for the winning edge, has replaced Earl Morrall with a recuperated but rusty Bob Griese. Having driven to the Miami 7 before stalling out, the Steelers are back on top as the result of a 14-yard field goal by Roy Gerela. Score: 10-7.

This is Griese's first drive and reflects the effects of weeks of inactivity. He's calling a very cautious game. Despite having taken long warmups at halftime and during the Steelers' drive, he's not thrown thus far. Jim Kiick and Larry Csonka are at the running-back positions. This again is an indicator that Shula and Griese would like to remain ground-oriented.

Griese, however, is now in his first clutch situation. It's third and 6 at his own 24-yard line. What will be the strategy here? Will Griese risk a downfield pass? Or will he throw a flare pass to Kiick—a Kiick specialty. Will he pass at all? He's had no real work at quarterbacking since the fifth game of the season. The Steeler defense has allowed Morrall, before departing in favor of Griese, 7 completions in 11 attempts. But none was very spectacular, and the combined yardage isn't that great. Does Griese feel that he is up to throwing under these circumstances, or will be call a running play and then punt, if need be?

CALL YOUR PLAY:

1. Have Kiick swing out of the backfield for a pass. Shula often inserts Kiick into the line-up on third down for this reason. Will the move be overlooked by the Steeler defense?

2. Hope to surprise the Steeler secondary by not only throwing, but by throwing deep and to a wide receiver. How about Paul Warfield on a look-in in the middle zone?

3. Call a quarterback sneak, but bring Morrall back in to run it.

4. Run Csonka on a conservative smack at the right flank of the Steelers. Miami uses this play often and well.

AFC PLAYOFF 1972

PLAY #3

Just after giving up the first down on a penalty, the Steeler defense stiffens at its 13-yard line. As if to atone for wiping out Jack Ham's prior interception, Steeler defensive end Dwight White blows in on the first play of the series to drop Larry Csonka, slanting over left tackle behind the blocking of Miami's giant tackle Wayne Moore, for a yard loss. With second and 11, Griese goes to tight end Marv Fleming with a look-in for 9 yards, which gets down to the 5. This time on third down, Griese gives to Jim Kiick over All-Pro Larry Little's right-guard position. The tackle is credited to safeties Mike Wagner and Glen Edwards, showing how the Steeler defense reacts, but still the gain is only a yard's worth. Granted, the Steeler secondary is pinched in and up, but being stopped by two safeties after only a yard pick-up tells something about the defensive unit.

Griese is now in a position to exercise his grasp of the mental side of professional football. Fourth and 1 is the situation. Will Miami take a field goal? It would make the score 10-10. Or will Griese go for a touchdown-producing play? The needed yard, if gotten, would give the Dolphins a first and goal at the Steelers' 3-yard line. From there it would take a superhuman effort on the part of the "Steel Curtain" to keep Csonka & Co. out of the end zone. The touchdown, if produced, would give Miami a 14-10 lead and give their defensive platoon a real "cushion" in dealing with the Steeler offense and Terry Hanratty. Don Shula's club is too sound a group to take many gambles, but they are behind now and have a great chance to exercise the option of going for it or kicking. Will this play be the one on which Shula looks for the winning edge?

CALL YOUR PLAY:

1. Take the tying field goal. Garo Yepremian would be lofting an 11-yarder.

2. Send Csonka over left tackle behind Norm Evans' block, with guard Bob Kuchenberg supplying additional firepower.

3. Come back with Jim Kiick over right tackle, taking advantage of strong blocking by tight end Marv Fleming, tackle Wayne Moore, and guard Larry Little.

4. Test Griese's ankle with a quarterback sneak.

Super Perfect

SUPER BOWL VII
January 14, at Los Angeles
(Attendance 90,182)

The contrasts were interesting. The Miami Dolphins had swept through fourteen regular-season games and two playoff games without a loss and now had a chance to compile a perfect 17-0 record for the year. Under the thorough leadership of head coach Don Shula, the Dolphins had rebounded from last year's Super Bowl loss to Dallas to become a cool, mature club.

The Washington Redskins had mostly veteran players, but their style was not one of coolness. Coach George Allen strove to whip his men into a frenzy before every game, and he put a fanatical emphasis on this game. A loss in this game would spoil the entire season, he said, and he drilled his troops in Spartan fashion to prepare them for the younger Dolphins.

The Miami defense scuttled the Washington running attack right from the start, a reversal from last year's dissection of the Dolphin front wall by the Cowboys. Larry Brown and Charley Harraway found Miami tackle Manny Fernandez forever in their path, and quarterback Bill Kilmer suffered through a bad afternoon with his passing. The Dolphins picked off three passes, with safety Jake Scott making two of the interceptions.

The Dolphins attack moved well against the heralded Redskin defense, but three penalties prevented any score until late in the period. Just before the end of the quarter Howard Twilley beat Pat Fischer to the outside and hauled in a 28-yard Bob Griese touchdown pass which he carried in from the 5. Leading 7-0, the Dolphins continued to paralyze the Redskin offense in the second period and scored again late in the period. One minute before halftime Jim Kiick capped a long Miami drive by going over from the one-yard line, giving the Dolphins a solid 14-0 lead at intermission.

The Redskins finally got their offense rolling after taking the second-half kickoff. With Brown gaining on the ground and Kilmer completing three passes, the Redskins drove into Miami territory before the drive stalled. Curt Knight then lined up a comparatively easy 32-yard field goal, but his kick sailed wide to the right and the Dolphins took possession.

The Miami defense re-established its superiority through

the second half as the Dolphin offense held onto the ball long enough on each possession to eat up valuable time. With two minutes left in the game, Garo Yepremian attempted a 42-yard field goal, only to have it blocked. When the ball bounced back to him, he picked it up and started to run toward the sidelines. With no football experience except kicking, Yepremian then attempted to pass the ball, only to have it slip out of his hands right to Mike Bass of the Redskins. Bass ran 49 yards with the aborted pass for Washington's only score of the day, but the Dolphins hung onto the 14-7 lead.

SUPER BOWL VII

MIAMI	**7**	**7**	**0**	**0-14**
WASHINGTON	**0**	**0**	**0**	**7- 7**

First Quarter

Miami	Twilley, 28 yard pass from Griese PAT — Yepremian (kick	14:59

Second Quarter

Miami	Kiick, 1 yard rush PAT — Yepremian (kick)	14:42

Fourth Quarter

Was.	Bass, 49 yard fumble return PAT — Knight	12:53

TEAM STATISTICS

MIAMI		**WASH.**
12	First Downs — Total	16
7	First Downs — Rushing	9
5	First Downs — Passing	7
0	First Downs — Penalty	0
2	Fumbles — Number	1
1	Fumbles — Lost Ball	0
3	Penalties — Number	3
35	Yards Penalized	25
50	Total Offensive Plays	66
253	Total Net Yards	228
5.1	Average Gain	3.5
1	Missed Field Goals	1
2	Giveaways	3
3	Takeaways	2
+1	Difference	−1

SUPER BOWL VII

PLAY #1

There is no score in the game, and Miami and Washingtor are really just sparring with each other in the first period. Each team has had the ball twice with nothing to show for it. Now Miami is grinding out yardage on a drive featuring "Butch Cassidy and 'The Sundance Kid,' " or Larry Csonkɛ and Jim Kiick, if you prefer. Occasionally, the rapidl maturing Bob Griese will throw to the man considered b many to be *the* premier wide receiver in football, Pau Warfield. On this drive, no matter who or what Griese uses it seems to work. Griese's got the club down to the Redskins 28-yard line, but the numbers are third and 4.

The Skins, like all teams coached by George Allen, ar defensively oriented. This is not to say they don't have a offense—any team with a Larry Brown, a Charley Taylor and a Roy Jefferson is bound to be "offensive." But Alle has brought in the likes of Jack Pardee and Ron McDole t give himself a mature and experienced defensive team. It' this mature aspect that has earned the club the nickname o "The Over-the-Hill Gang." Regardless of past performances the "gang" is having trouble containing Miami, a club unde feated in regular and postseason play—16 wins and 0 losses During the course of the season, the Dolphs have had som close calls, but they've always managed to pull the game ou This is especially commendable when you consider that Bo Griese missed most of the season with a broken ankle, th gracefully aging Earl Morrall filling in for him. Howeve Griese is at the helm of the Miami attack now and is attemptir to get into the end zone before Washington does. Wi several weapons from which to choose, what will his call be

CALL YOUR PLAY:

1. "Go for the downs" by throwing deep to Howard Twilley running a flag pattern to the right side where diminutive Pat Fischer defends.

2. Run a sneak to the middle of the field to set up a field goal.

3. Run Csonka on a basic running play for the first down.

4. As he has done so often in the past, have Shula send in Jim Kiick and throw to him coming out of the backfield. Kiick is particularly adept at this.

SUPER BOWL VII

PLAY #2

Behind by the most lopsided 14-0 score in memory, the Redskins need to get something going. Miami's "No Names" have harassed Washington quarterback Billy Kilmer all day and have made Larry Brown pay the price for what relatively little yardage he is getting. While all Miami defenders are very effective, Manny Fernandez is having the kind of day most defensive tackles would only dare dream about. The comparatively small tackle—6'2" and 248 pounds (stack those figures up against a Buck Buchanan)—is playing the run so well that John Wilbur, the oft-victimized right guard of the Skins, is on the verge of becoming a household word.

Fernandez is also mounting a pressing pass-rush. Whatever play Kilmer selects, it will have to be done with respect to the kind of game the Dolphins' left defensive tackle is playing.

A drive, which began on the Redskins' 11-yard line now has progressed to the Miami 10-yard line. Kilmer is passing for a respectable percentage, but he is not really getting the yardage he needs when he needs it most. Also, for want of someone better to blame, "the Fates" are treating the Skins with less than kindness. On the previous down (second) Kilmer was in need of 6 yards, he not only seemed to have that, but it appeared for an instant that Kilmer had his fine tight end, Jerry Smith, open for a much-needed touchdown. But Kilmer's pass was thrown on a trajectory that intersected with the goal post and not the fast-moving Smith. The ball bounced harmlessly away as it struck the upright. Now Kilmer has a problem on third and 6. What can he do to get a positive reaction from his offensive mates? They must be close to totally disappointed by the cruel twist of the last play. Will he again go for the touchdown or attempt to get first-down yardage, settling for a field goal on fourth down, if all else fails?

CALL YOUR PLAY:

1. Try the same play, since Smith was open, but throw a little sooner to avoid the goal post.

2. Call a draw play with Larry Brown going up the middle. This would take advantage of Fernandez' all-out charge on a suspected pass.

3. Try to split the Miami "zone" by going to Charley Taylor on a post pattern between right cornerback Lloyd Mumphord and right safety Jake Scott.

4. Hand off to Charlie Harraway, figuring Miami will be looking for Larry Brown.

SUPER BOWL VII

PLAY #3

If the Redskins seemed to be mathematically close when it was 14-0, they are now even closer, mathematically, at 14-7. The closeness of the score is the result of what will probably always be regarded as the wildest play in Super Bowl history. It was the play that kicker Garo Yepremian turned passer—almost. The net result was Mike Bass's 49-yard touchdown run with Garo's "air ball." The time remaining in the game is vital now—only 2:07 to play.

Head coach George Allen is now faced with a decision difficult enough to warrant the salary and recognition an NFC coach gets—what to do on the ensuing kickoff. It's tough enough for the Skins to score with the ball today. It will be even tougher without. Somehow Washington has got to get the ball back and get it back quickly. It would also be in their best interests if they can prevent Miami from using much time or from having to call time-outs of their own.

In a situation such as this, there may seem to be only one way to go, but the fertile football mind of Allen is undoubtedly weighing options that the average person is not even aware of. An onside kick seems to be the only route to take, but is it? And how best to work it, if it is the call Allen decides on. Will it be a rather conventional kick with the speedsters up front to recover it? Will it be some as yet unseen innovation that Allen is saving for just such a time? Who's to say George Allen will go for the onside kick at all. If it fails, there is time for Miami to march for a field goal that would make any Washington touchdown purely academic. Maybe Allen has a special defense that will take the ball away from Miami down deep in Dolphin territory.

CALL YOUR PLAY:

1. Follow the advice of 90,000 grandstand quarterbacks and countless armchair quarterbacks and kick off onside.

2. Kick off deep in the normal manner and take your chances on stopping Miami, getting the ball back with time enough, and eventually scoring.

3. Squib-kick medium distance and try to recover with a fast "bomb-squadder."

4. Squib-kick medium distance, hoping the odd rotation of the ball and the pressure of the moment will cause the dolphins to commit a turnover.

1973

NFC PLAYOFF 1973

DALLAS	**0**	**0**	**10**	**0-10**
MINNESOTA	**3**	**7**	**7**	**10-27**

First Quarter

Minn.	Cox, 44-yard field goal

Second Quarter

Minn.	Foreman, 5 yard rush PAT — Cox (kick)

Third Quarter

Dall.	Richards, 63 yard punt return PAT — Fritsch (kick)
Minn.	Gilliam, 54 yard pass from Tarkenton PAT — Cox (kick)
Dall.	Fritsch, 17 yard field goal

Fourth Quarter

Minn.	Bryant, 63 yard interception return PAT — Cox (kick)
Minn.	Cox, 34 yard field goal

TEAM STATISTICS

DALLAS		MINN.
9	First Downs — Total	20
3	First Downs — Rushing	14
5	First Downs — Passing	6
1	First Downs — Penalty	0
2	Fumbles — Number	4
2	Fumbles — Lost Ball	3
2	Penalties — Number	3
20	Yards Penalized	33
0	Missed Field Goals	0
49	Offensive Plays	72
153	Net Yards	306
3.1	Average Gain	4.3
6	Giveaways	4
4	Takeaways	6
−2	Difference	+2

NFC PLAYOFF 1973

PLAY #1

As the game unfolds, Roger Staubach begins probing the Viking defense. The front four of Carl Eller and Jim Marshall at ends, and Alan Page and Gary Larsen at tackles, is regarded as one of the best of all time, but Staubach shows no partiality. Using underslung Robert Newhouse, who will have to shoulder the burden of the running game with Calvin Hill on the bench injured, the Cowboy offense is directed over left guard, around right end, and up the middle on Staubach scrambles. A first down is netted, but the drive sputters and Minnesota gets the ball at its own 39-yard line.

Minnesota attacks the usual spots—Chuck Foreman going over right tackle, behind Ron Yary, and Oscar Reed blasting up the middle—but something different is going on. The Dallas defense (like that of the great New York Giants of the 1950s and early 1960s) is predicated on keeping the blockers away from and off of the middle linebacker (Lee Roy Jordan is the Dallas middleman, Sam Huff was the Giants' "meg" man), allowing him to read, react, and make the tackle. Minnesota is running "sucker" plays or "misdirection" now. In the past, if the Minnesota left guard (huge and powerful Ed White) would pull, the ball would be given to the running back stationed on the left side of the offensive set. Today, Tarkenton is handing off to the other back going toward the hole left by the pulling guard. This is something which would show up in a report from a prior game; but it hasn't, and the Dallas defense, Jordan in particular, is having some trouble adjusting.

With no score, Minnesota is moving well, but the drive faces a fourth and 1 (actually inches) at the Dallas 17-yard line. On the previous play, a third and 1, Foreman was stopped short.

CALL YOUR PLAY:

1. Scoring first is important in any game. Scoring first in a championship game is doubly important. Take the 24-yard field goal.

2. Run Oscar Reed on a "misdirection" at left guard where White has pulled out, leaving no blocking, but hopefully a ready-made hole.

3. Pass into the end zone on a flag pattern on the left side of the end zone.

4. Roll out, running or passing as indicated by the situation.

NFC PLAYOFF 1973

PLAY #2

Early in the second quarter Minnesota is moving again. Tarkenton is beginning to set the pattern for the game. He's throwing frequently on first down, having great success doing it. Later in a locker-room interview, Viking coach Bud Grant will say, "I didn't realize Fran was throwing so much on first down. It wasn't part of our game plan." Nevertheless, Minnesota is moving in a manner that belies their reputation as the methodical, plodding giants from the north country.

With a first and 10 at his own 14-yard line, the result of a long Dallas punt by Marv Bateman, Tarkenton calmly stepped back, surveyed the situation downfield, and calmly threw a completion to Stu Voight, his tight end, who is becoming a valued receiver in the Minnesota ball-control scheme of things. It was good for 16 yards and another first down. Getting out of the conservative "bag," Tarkenton continued to move the club downfield. Only about 30 yards away from another touchdown, Tarkenton is facing his second moment of decision. After Oscar Reed is stopped a yard short on third and 2, Fran looks over a measurement by the officials.

He sizes it up, holds up his left hand with his thumb and forefinger an inch or so apart, and signals to the bench. He gets a signal and goes into the huddle to make the call. Will they go for it again? Will they take an immediate field goal by Fred Cox? It would be a 35-yard attempt by the stocky Pitt grad, and since he already has booted one from 44 yards out, this would seem a sure 3 points. Do the Vikes want another three or are they hungry for more. Will the Cowboys have anything to say about what happens?

CALL YOUR PLAY:

1. Run Reed over left guard on the "sucker" play. It's been working well.

2. Have Tarkenton roll out left.

3. Stay away from the "sucker" play and bang away with Foreman over right guard.

4. Take Fred Cox's try at a 35-yard field goal.

NFC PLAYOFF 1973

PLAY #3

Minnesota is having great success with its revamped offense. They continue to "work" on middle linebacker Lee Roy Jordan. The game plan includes the "misdirections" and "suckers" mentioned earlier and passes at unexpected times by Viking quarterback Fran Tarkenton. Minnesota is still working away from Dallas's pursuing defense, even though All-Pro Bob Lilly is out with a back injury—something that has bothered him all season long. Basic football strategy dictates running right at the defense to cut its effectiveness at pursuit. This is the best tactic to use when dealing with an active defense such as Dallas's. It is also the way teams attack Minnesota's own Alan Page—with varying degrees of success, it might be added.

Dallas has had little to cheer about thus far, but even though Minnesota is truly the dominant team, the Cowboys are close on the scoreboard by virtue of Golden Richards' blazing 63-yard punt return. Fran Tarkenton has been throwing a great deal in first-down situations, something he didn't do during the regular season. Of the 21 passes he'll throw, 11 of them will be on first down, and a significant number of these will be completed. This and the "sucker" plays aimed at Jordan's quick reactions have the Dallas defense still somewhat off balance.

On two quick plays Tarkenton has a first down at his own 46-yard line. Stung by Richards' long return, will Tarkenton go with the pass again on first down? Could a deep throw be expected in this situation, and if it is, will Dallas be ready for it—perhaps intercepting and getting back into a game they appeared to be losing?

CALL YOUR PLAY:

1. Go for the old tried-and-true "misdirect" with Foreman going up the middle.

2. Throw a "home run" to John Gilliam deep on a fly pattern.

3. Cross them up with the Statue of Liberty.

4. Have Tarkenton call a sneak, just to give Dallas something to think about.

AFC PLAYOFF 1973

MIAMI	**7**	**7**	**3**	**10-27**
OAKLAND	**0**	**0**	**10**	**0-10**

First Quarter		
Miami	Csonka, 11 yard rush	
		PAT — Yepremian (kick)
Second Quarter		
Miami	Csonka, 2 yard rush	
		PAT — Yepremian (kick)
Third Quarter		
Oak.	Blanda, 21 yard field goal	
Miami	Yepremian, 42 yard field goal	
Oak.	Siani, 25 yard pass from Stabler	
		PAT — Blanda (kick)
Fourth Quarter		
Miami	Yepremian, 26 yard field goal	
Miami	Csonka, 2 yard rush	
		PAT — Yepremian (kick)

TEAM STATISTICS

MIAMI		OAK.
21	First Downs — Total	15
18	First Downs — Rushing	4
2	First Downs — Passing	8
1	First Downs — Penalty	2
1	Fumbles — Number	1
0	Fumbles — Lost Ball	0
3	Penalties — Number	3
26	Yards Penalized	35
0	Missed Field Goals	1
60	Offensive Plays	49
292	Net Yards	236
4.9	Average Gain	4.8
1	Giveaways	1
1	Takeaways	1
0	Difference	0

AFC PLAYOFF 1973

PLAY #1

The Oakland Raiders are being picked apart very methodically on a Bob Griese-led, ball-control drive. The Miami ground game has been so effective that Oakland isn't on the scoreboard, and it's the third quarter of play. Larry Csonka and Mercury Morris are gouging the Oakland defense repeatedly. The ball-control strategy usually doesn't produce many points; but a good drive can kill most of a quarter, and if it produces a touchdown, it is a very effective device. Miami has done this once in each of the first two quarters.

In the second half Oakland starts to move. Left-handed quarterback Kenny Stabler is passing effectively, even if the points aren't being hung up on the scoreboard. Marv Hubbard, keyed up by the prospects of dueling head-to-head with Csonka, and Charlie Smith are running fairly well, but the Oakland Raiders just have not had the ball long enough to be very productive.

Now things are jelling. Stabler has the Raiders deep in Miami territory, but it's a crucial situation—fourth and 4 at the 14-yard line. There are much better spots to be in for a coach or a quarterback. Do the Raiders have the confidence in their offensive unit to go for it? Are they sure enough of it to take the low-risk field-goal attempt now and make other scoring drives later? This is a decision that has to be made now. And if the choice is to go for the first down and the touchdown, a play with a high degree of success built into it it will have to be called. John Madden will earn his pay on this play. Time is not a vital factor, but a trend in the game can be set, one way or the other, on this play.

CALL YOUR PLAY:

1. Roll out left and throw or run as the Miami defense presents itself.

2. Call a draw play up the middle with Marv Hubbard getting the ball after the fake pass.

3. Play it close to the vest and get the points as they present themselves: have George Blanda kick the 21-yard field goal.

4. Bring in Pete Banaszak for his specialty—getting the tough yards. Run him off the right side on a slant inside the end.

Dolphin Defense and Csonka Crashes

SUPER BOWL VIII
January 13, at Houston
(Attendance 68,142)

The Dolphins did not enjoy a perfect season this year, but they did play an almost perfect game against the Vikings in the Super Bowl. After receiving the opening kickoff, the Dolphins immediately set the tone of the day with a crunching 62-yard drive. With the Miami line ripping the famous Minnesota front four to shreds, Larry Csonka repeatedly burst through the middle for good yardage. On the tenth play of the drive, Csonka bulled into the end zone from five yards out; the Dolphins now had a 7-0 lead to nurse.

The Miami Dolphins did not stop with their seven-point lead. With Bob Griese passing very rarely, the Miami attack continued to move the ball on the ground. The Dolphin linemen habitually beat the Viking front four off the ball, slamming into them before they could react; Minnesota ends Carl Eller and Jim Marshall were taken out of almost every play. The second Dolphin touchdown came late in the opening quarter on a plunge by Jim Kiick, who had not scored all season. Garo Yepremian added the extra point, and the 14-0 lead looked close to impregnable.

Yepremian added a field goal in the second quarter to give the Dolphins a 17-0 halftime edge that understated the one-sidedness of the first half. The Vikings were not making out-and-out blunders; they simply were being beaten by better blocking and tackling. They did make a mistake on the second-half kickoff when a clipping penalty called back a long return by John Gilliam. The momentum which the return had given to the Vikings immediately shifted back to the Dolphins, and within seven minutes Csonka drove into the end zone.

With the decision no longer in doubt, the Vikings got onto the scoreboard in the fourth quarter on a touchdown run by Tarkenton. After Cox booted the extra point, the Vikings shocked Miami by recovering an on-side kick; once again, however, a penalty nullified the play and nipped a Minnesota rally before it could begin.

By the end of the day, the Dolphins again were undisputed champions of pro football, and Larry Csonka had set a Super Bowl rushing record with 145 hard-fought yards. With two straight championships to their credit, the Dolphins now drew comparisons with the Packers of Vince Lombardi's era.

Marv Fleming, who played on both clubs, said, "This is the greatest team ever."

SUPER BOWL VIII

MIAMI	**14**	**3**	**7**	**0-24**
MINNESOTA	**0**	**0**	**0**	**7- 7**

First Quarter		
Miami	Csonka, 5 yard rush PAT — Yepremian (kick)	9:33
Miami	Kiick, 1 yard rush PAT — Yepremian (kick)	13:38
Second Quarter		
Miami	Yepremian, 28 yard field goal	8:58
Third Quarter		
Miami	Csonka, 2 yard rush PAT — Yepremian (kick)	6:16
Fourth Quarter		
Minn.	Tarkenton, 4 yard rush PAT — Cox (kick)	1:35

TEAM STATISTICS

MIAMI		MINN.
21	First Downs — Total	14
13	First Downs — Rushing	5
4	First Downs — Passing	8
4	First Downs — Penalty	1
1	Fumbles — Number	2
0	Fumbles — Lost Ball	1
1	Penalties — Number	7
4	Yards Penalized	65
0	Missed Field Goals	0
61	Offensive Plays	54
259	Net Yards	238
4.2	Average Gain	4.4
0	Giveaways	2
2	Takeaways	0
+2	Difference	−2

SUPER BOWL VIII

PLAY #1

Miami is thoroughly dominating the early going, allowing Minnesota just 3 plays for 9 yards, while scoring themselves on a time-consuming 5½ minute drive after the opening kickoff. As the first period is fading, the Dolphins are again grinding out consistent, if not spectacular gains. Larry Csonka and Mercury Morris, with an occasional blast by Jim Kiick and a well-timed Bob Griese pass, are marching Miami dangerously close to the Minnesota goal again.

On first and 10, Kiick is dumped by Alan Page, Minnesota's superb defensive tackle, for a 3-yard loss, but Csonka has picked up the slack for "Sundance" by getting back these 3 yards and another 9 on a sweep to the right. Larry Little, as good an offensive guard as Page is a defensive tackle, and Norm Evans, a steady performer at offensive tackle, provided the key blocks.

Thus far, the offensive line—center Jim Langer, guard Bob Kuchenburg, tackle Wayne Moore, and tight end Jim Mandich are the other members of the cast—is getting the best of it in their "pit" battle with the "Purple People-Eaters." They are helped by Griese's selection of "misdirection" plays. This type of play pulls a lineman out of the line, as if to lead a wide play, and then punches the back through the hole left by the offensive lineman. For the play to work well, the defender has to be influenced by the pulling lineman and the reverse flow of the other members of the backfield. This is happening. On a third and 1, Csonka busts a stacked Minnesota defense for 8 yards. It seems Griese can send his backs through the line as he chooses. Now he has first and 10 at the Vikes' 14-yard line. Will he continue the overland route? Or is now the time to "zing" Minnesota with one of the 7 passes that he will throw all day (he'll complete all but 1 of them)?

CALL YOUR PLAY:

1. Call a Statue of Liberty with Mercury Morris coming back to the right and taking the deep handoff.

2. Pull Bob Kuchenberg on the "misdirection" and send Csonka through the "hole."

3. Now is the time to go to Paul Warfield for the "quick six."

4. Continue to ignore Warfield and throw deep to Marlin Briscoe, as Griese has done successfully before.

SUPER BOWL VIII

PLAY #2

Two sustained Miami drives and a field goal have put the Vikings behind 17-0 early int he game—a familiar situation to most of the AFC teams—and the Miami defense has successfully contained the Vikings' scrambling quarterback. Tarkenton is running, looking, and throwing, but he is not having one of his finer days. This is not unusual when a quarterback faces Miami. Not only have the Dolphin defenders done the job on Tarkenton, they have virtually closed down the running game of Chuck Foreman, Bill Brown, Ed Marinaro, and Oscar Reed. No one seems to know exactly what the game plan of Minnesota is, but it doesn't seem to be working very well.

But now, Fran Tarkenton has his club within striking distance. Passing mainly to his tight end Stu Voight and wide receiver John Gilliam, he has moved the club inside the Dolphin 10-yard line. After getting 8 yards himself on a rollout right, he has fed to running back Oscar Reed on two successive plays but has only netted an additional yard. With exactly a minute to play in the half and Minnesota needing a score, Tarkenton is faced with a fourth and 1 (actually it is only 3 inches) at the Miami 6-yard line. A field goal from Fred Cox would be almost a certainty, but do the Vikes want more? With an entire half to play, their formidable defense could hold Miami, and if Tarkenton gets untracked, two or more touchdowns are not an impossibility. Is the field goal—following the theory that you better take something when you can—the only option open to Bud Grant's team? Those 3 inches look very inviting.

CALL YOUR PLAY:

1. Send the field goal unit on, and kick. Cox's try would be from 13-yards away.

2. Gamble on the "inches" with Tarkenton rolling out, keeping if the Dolphins hang back, passing if they come up to meet him.

3. Give to Reed on a slant at right tackle, figuring that the big running back can't be held to virtually nothing on three straight plays. Also, he'd be following Ron Yary's block.

4. Throw deep into the end zone to John Gilliam on a flag pattern.

SUPER BOWL VIII

PLAY #3

In the final period Fran Tarkenton gets a Viking score on a quicker version of a typical Miami drive—ten plays covering 57 yards, but in just 3 minutes and 9 seconds. Relying on the pass, he moved to the 4-yard line and from there circled right end on a keeper for the six-pointer.

There is still 13:25 remaining in the game—lots of time in a run-of-the-mill game—but except for this just-completed drive by Minnesota, Miami has really controlled the game. With virtually no running game, the Vikes' quarterback is forced to live by his wits in dealing with a Miami defense that seems to be included in the Vikings' offensive huddle—they are that effective. While Tarkenton is completing a high percentage of his passes, they are, for the most part, going to his running backs and tight ends and not really doing much damage to Miami's tough zone defense. Now, with some points to their name, if the Viking defense is able to turn in several "three and out" series to get the ball back for the offensive platoon, quick scores by Tarkenton & Co. could pull out the game.

But can the Vikes strike quickly? Thus far, scrambling Fran has presented the Miami "No Names" with no unsolvable problems. Can they afford to give Miami the ball at all? The alternative seems to be an onside kick. At best, they are risky, but will coach Bud Grant take the gamble? Down by a 24-7 count, Grant appears to have no choice but to attempt the kick. His real choice seems to be how to effect the kick and the recovery—short, medium, or what? Should he do as George Allen did a year earlier versus the Dolphs, and if so, what will his strategy be on playing it "straight"? Will he stick with basics and hope, or does he have something more in keeping with the circumstances?

CALL YOUR PLAY:

1. Kick off onside, but decoy it by not using all ball-handlers (defensive backs, wide receivers, tight ends, and running backs) on the kickoff team.

2. Kick off onside, but don't be cute. Use your best men for the play, cutting down on the surprise element, but giving your chances of success a boost.

3. Kick away deep and rely on the newly awakening Minnesota Viking defense to stop Miami.

4. Kick away, but instruct Cox to "squib" the ball, making it hard to handle and increasing the likelihood of a Miami turnover.

1974

NFC PLAYOFF 1974

MINNESOTA	**0**	**7**	**0**	**7-14**
LOS ANGELES	**0**	**3**	**0**	**7-10**

Second Quarter

Minn.	Lash, 29 yard pass from Tarkenton PAT — Cox (kick)
L.A.	Ray, 27 yard field goal

Fourth Quarter

Minn.	Osborn, 1 yard rush PAT — Cox (kick)
L.A.	Jackson, 44 yard pass from Harris PAT — Ray (kick)

TEAM STATISTICS

MINN.		L.A
18	First Downs — Total	15
9	First Downs — Rushing	5
7	First Downs — Passing	10
2	First Downs — Penalty	0
5	Fumbles — Number	3
2	Fumbles — Lost Ball	3
2	Penalties — Number	7
20	Yards Penalized	70
0	Missed Field Goals	0
69	Offensive Plays	58
269	Net Yards	340
3.9	Average Gain	5.
3	Giveaways	5
5	Takeaways	3
+2	Difference	−2

NFC PLAYOFF 1974

PLAY #1

In the first quarter neither Los Angeles nor Minnesota did much to aid its own cause, but considerable to help the other club. There were back-to-back fumbles (each resulting in a change of possession), a 27-yard punt, dropped passes, interceptions, and enough errors to qualify the teams for Super Bowl V. With all this, still the first quarter was scoreless. The second quarter continues in the same vane.

Francis Tarkenton is directing the Minnesota attack. It consists mostly of plays run inside the tackles. While "do-everything" Chuck Foreman would seem like the man to lean on, Tarkenton is actually running steady Dave Osborn most of the time. Fran is running more than throwing. Here again he is staying away from Foreman (also deep-threat wide receiver John Gilliam) and has not mounted anything close to a serious scoring threat. The passes he's thrown are going to tight end Stu Voight and Dave Osborn. He's aimed a couple in the direction of young Jim Lash, his other wide receiver, but the results are nothing spectacular.

Taking over on their own 40-yard line after a Los Angeles punt, Minnesota has another chance to get something cranked up. On first and 10 Foreman is stopped for no gain. Then two misses and two catches get the ball to the Rams' 31-yard line with a first and 10. Tark goes back to the run and Osborn gets 2. On second and 8 Tarkenton can do several things, but it would be best to do something to maintain the momentum Minnesota now has. Will he use Foreman or Gilliam—his heaviest weapons? Or will the call be something else—more dramatic or more conservative? The weather and field conditions really shouldn't dictate play. It's a balmy 30 degrees in Bloomington this day, and the field is in fine condition considering the locale and time of the year.

CALL YOUR PLAY:

1. Roll out right, with Tark keeping or throwing as the defense dictates.

2. Go with proven success. Run Foreman over right tackle behind the blocking of Ron Yary.

3. Have Foreman throw an option pass to tight end Stu Voight crossing into the middle.

4. Figuring they will be looking for Gilliam on any deep pass that might be attempted, "decoy" him and go to Jim Lash. Throw against the Rams' right side.

NFC PLAYOFF 1974

PLAY #2

With a 7-3 halftime score favoring Minnesota, the "comedy of errors" moves into the second and final act. The script is still pretty much the same. In fact, the score is the same at the end of the third period as it was at halftime.

Now Minnesota is in the middle of what they hope will be a long, sustained, time-consuming drive. Tarkenton, getting the ball at the 20-yard line, has moved steadily upfield. Chuck Foreman is getting the call oftener, and producing. Osborn is his steady self, getting what's needed. Tark is hitting all his receivers on a variety of patterns, and Los Angeles is helping with an ill-timed penalty that cost them a "sack" of Tarkenton. The Vikes move to a first down and goal-to-go at the 7-yard line, but things are coming very easy for them. Two shots by Foreman and a Tarkenton scramble still leave Minnesota outside the end zone, but the distance is only 1 inch to go.

Time has ticked down to less than 10 minutes, and Los Angeles has shown a penchant for stopping itself—remember the 98-yard drive for no points? Surely, coach Bud Grant's Vikings will go for the touchdown here. Won't they? There are lots of ways to make an inch, but in this game it better be the right way. Maybe a field goal is the answer. Cox would have an easy shot at it. Actually, it would amount to kicking a point-after-touchdown. The score would go to 10-3, and the Rams would still only manage a tie game if they scored a touchdown themselves. These are all factors to be taken into account before settling on a play for "fourth and inches."

CALL YOUR PLAY:

1. It's becoming a cliché, but—try for it by "sending Foreman over right tackle behind Ron Yary's blocking."

2. Have Tarkenton roll out again, but run into the end zone with no intention of passing.

3. Call Osborn off left guard, figuring they'll be looking for Foreman behind Yary at right tackle.

4. Take the Fred Cox field goal.

NFC PLAYOFF 1974

PLAY #3

Minnesota kicks off and now the Los Angeles Rams are in a "must" situation. With just over 12 minutes to play and vivid memories of so many frustrations, the Rams have got to get it together, especially since they need more than a touchdown and a field goal to win.

Cullen Bryant returns a relatively short kickoff 25 yards to the Rams' 35-yard line, and James Harris sets up. His first play—a pass to tight end Bob Klein, who is emerging as "more than just a blocker"—gets a first down. Heisman trophy winner, John Cappelletti is in the Rams' backfield now, and he dents the Minnesota line for 5 yards. The Rams are moving, but so is the clock. A quicker way of covering the needed ground is called for. Harris hands off to Lawrence McCutcheon, his 1000-yard rusher, for 1 yard, and then passes to Cappellett for 5 and a first down.

The ball is now at the Vikings' 44-yard line. Can the Ram afford this kind of a drive? Middle-distance passes and runnin plays aren't normal calls for a team playing "catch up." Harris is passing fairly well, even if he doesn't have much t show for it in the way of points. But then, how often do yo complete a 73-yard pass that is not a touchdown and sti manage not to score any points? Do the Rams have enoug confidence in their passing game to throw on first down? If sc will it be a deep pass or something on the shorter side? Sho is safe, but will this tactic leave enough time to get the point needed to win? Remember, the Vikings' front four of Jir Marshall, Carl Eller, Alan Page, and Doug Sutherland ar getting older, but they are still a pretty savage unit to wor against, especially when they have a pretty good idea c what's coming. Assuming there is no turnover, passing earl would give the Rams more opportunities.

CALL YOUR PLAY:

1. Go deep to Jack Snow, who caught the only pass throw to him so far today for a 19-yard gain. Send him down th left sideline.

2. Go deep to Harold Jackson, angling in toward th middle on a deep post pattern.

3. Run McCutcheon to set up something for later.

4. Harris is a strong athlete. Call a rollout right.

AFC PLAYOFF 1974

OAKLAND	**3**	**0**	**7**	**3-13**
PITTSBURGH	**0**	**3**	**0**	**21-24**

First Quarter
Oak. Blanda, 40 yard field goal

Second Quarter
Pitt. Gerela, 23 yard field goal

Third Quarter
Oak. Branch, 38 yard pass from Stabler
PAT — Blanda (kick)

Fourth Quarter
Pitt. Harris, 8 yard rush
PAT — Gerela (kick)
Pitt. Swann, 6 yard pass from Bradshaw
PAT — Gerela (kick)
Oak. Blanda, 24 yard field goal
Pitt. Harris, 21 yard rush
PAT — Gerela (kick)

TEAM STATISTICS

OAK.		PITT.
15	First Downs — Total	20
0	First Downs — Rushing	11
13	First Downs — Passing	7
2	First Downs — Penalty	2
0	Fumbles — Number	3
0	Fumbles — Lost Ball	2
5	Penalties — Number	4
60	Yards Penalized	30
1	Missed Field Goals	1
59	Offensive Plays	68
278	Net Yards	35
4.7	Average Gain	4.5
3	Giveaways	3
3	Takeaways	3
0	Difference	0

AFC PLAYOFF 1974

PLAY #1

Coming into the game, the Steelers were given little chanc to beat Oakland. They were blown away by the Raiders i the first-round playoffs last season. They were shut out 17- in the regular season in their own ballpark (and the gam wasn't as close as the score indicates). They were now on th road against an Oakland team (tough anywhere, but nearl unbeatable at Oakland-Alameda County Coliseum) that de feated Miami a week ago in spectacular fashion.

What little chance was given the Steelers was due to thei total route of the Buffalo Bills in the first round of the playoffs The "Steel Curtain" was the "Steel Curtain." Franco Harri was Franco Harris. And Rocky Bleier was acting like a scaled down model of Bronko Nagurski. But the big difference wa the newly established leadership provided the offense b Terry Bradshaw. Against Buffalo he was flawless. Agains Oakland, thus far, he was creditable, but the Steelers weren' getting any points. They weren't giving up much either– only 3 on a 40-yard George Blanda field goal (a fumble punt return gave the Raiders another quick chance at a score but they couldn't convert).

In the 1973 playoff, Oakland ate up the Steeler righ defensive side. With Kenny Stabler, a left-hander at quarte back, Oakland runs to the left much more than most clubs But in this game, thanks to a new defensive alignment, Oaklan isn't running anywhere. Nevertheless, the "pride and poise" gang is still ahead 3-0. After getting to the Oakland 3-yar line, the Steelers saw a good chance drift away with Ro Gerela's fading field-goal attempt. As the second quarte unfolds, the Steelers are moving again. Except for back-to-bac passes to Johnny Stallworth and Larry Brown, Bradshaw ha moved the club from midfield to the Oakland 6-yard line b grinding it out—Bleier and Franco doing the grinding. No it's fourth and 2 at the Raider 6. Will the Steelers try anothe kick? Will they go for it?

CALL YOUR PLAY:

1. Fake a field goal, and have holder Bobby Walden pass to Larry Brown. Remember: unlike many teams, Pittsburgh's holder (Walden) is not a backup quarterback.

2. There is no wind. Have Gerela attempt the 23-yard kick.

3. Sweep to the right side. Have Franco carry behind the convoy of Bleier, right guard Gerry Mullins, and right tackle Gordon Gravelle.

4. Pass from the double-tight end formation on a look-in to Larry Brown.

AFC PLAYOFF 1974

PLAY #2

In the second half the Steelers continue to force Ken Stabler to do more throwing than he'd like. Marv Hubbard, regarded by many as second only to Larry Csonka as a power runner, is not very effective. His long run has been a 3-yarder. Pete Banaszak, the "old reliable" of the Oakland Raiders, is getting the best average, 2.5 yards, but he's only got three carries. Clarence Davis has carried nine times for 12 yards. He'll carry once more for a 4-yarder, which will stand as the day's longest Raider rushing attempt.

To illustrate what Joe Greene, L. C. Greenwood, Ernie Holmes, and Dwight White (with help from the secondary and linebackers) are doing to Oakland, look at Marv Hubbard's stats. Take away his 3-yard long gain, and he then nets only 3 yards on 6 carries. But missed opportunities, turnovers, an interception after the Steelers had a first and goal at the 8-yard line, and other mistakes find the Steelers down 10-3 as the 4th quarter opens.

Oakland got it's touchdown when 9.3 speedster Cliff Branch burned Mel Blount for a 38-yard catch for the score.

Pittsburgh answered this with a drive that had them at the Raider 8-yard line as the third period ended, and Franco Harris blasted the Oakland middle on the first play of the last period to tie it.

After the kickoff, Oakland once again tries to get something going. To begin the drive from his 27-yard line, Stabler gives to Hubbard. The defense strings this play out so well that safety Mike Wagner comes up to dump Hubbard for a 4-yard loss on the weak-side sweep. Davis gets 2 back, but a holding penalty moves them back to a first and 10 at the 30-yard line. Stabler passes on first down, but Jack Ham, Steelers' All-Pro linebacker, gets the ball and runs it to the Raider 9-yard line. Bradshaw comes on the field to try to get the clincher and put Oakland away. Two plays later it's third and goal at the 6. Will the "clincher" be replaced by a "take anything" field goal? Or worse, nothing?

CALL YOUR PLAY:

1. Lynn Swann has been ignored all day long as Bradshaw has gone to his running game mainly. Could Oakland be ignoring the outstanding rookie receiver too? Go to him on a "post" pattern for the touchdown.

2. Having just swept the left end for a loss of 2, come back with Franco over right tackle.

3. Call a draw play with Bleier carrying.

4. Have Bradshaw keep on a run up the middle.

AFC PLAYOFF 1974

PLAY #3

Right after the Steelres up the score to 17-10, Stabler begins to find the right combination. The Steelers' "stunt 4-3" defense has given up virtually nothing to the Raiders' ground game, and this has to have Oakland frustrated. John Madden will later say, "Our passing was enough to win but we couldn't get the run going.'' Perhaps Oakland was looking for the Steeler ''stack-over'' defense, which has Joe Greene and Ernie Holmes pinch in on the center—in this case, Jim Otto.

Now the Steelers have made another change, but will Ken Stabler be able to exploit it? Feeling that Cliff Branch was getting to much room to roam, defensive coordinator Bud Carson, in a move best called controversial, has lifted Mel Blount in favor of rookie Jimmy Allen. With a second and 6 at his 34-yard line, Stabler hits Branch at midfield, and Branch takes the ball to the Steeler 24-yard line. Immediately Stabler goes back to Branch, and he makes a 12-yard catch on Allen for a first and 10 at the 12-yard line.

A 1-yard pop by Hubbard and a third-down incompletion by ''the Snake'' give Oakland a fourth and 5 at the 7. There's more than a half a period left to go, but will the Raiders ever get into a position again so close to the Steeler goal? Do they go for the first down and a touchdown, or do they take a Blanda field-goal attempt and play for the touchdown later? If Blanda makes the field goal, it will still take a touchdown to win it. Would it be wise to call time out here and go to the sidelines for a conference to discuss all available information and decide on a play that would have the highest chance of working—say, a pass to Cliff Branch against the inexperienced Allen?

CALL YOUR PLAY:

1. Huddle with coach John Madden and his assistants and call a pass to Branch—a short square-out to the sideline in front of Allen.

2. Take the 24-yard field goal and worry about the points later.

3. Convoy Davis around the right end on a power-sweep.

4. Call a rollout left (remember Stabler is a southpaw) and keep or throw as it unfolds.

Rooney's 42-Year Reward

SUPER BOWL IX
January 12, at New Orleans
(Attendance 79,065)

This year's Super Bowl matchups included the Minnesot Vikings, twice losers of the NFL's big meal ticket, and th Pittsburgh Steelers, who were enjoying their first trip to th post season event. For the Vikings, already branded as a clu unable to win the big one, the game was a matter of professiona pride. The Steelers' motivation came from the fact that the had finally pocketed their first conference title since 1933 the year the franchise began.

Many of the past Super Bowls have been conservative an relatively dull games, Super Bowl IX was no exception as bot teams continued the same offensive pattern of trying to avoi costly mistakes rather than trying to break the game open In fact, the only score of the first half was a safety, with th Steelers getting two points when Viking quarterback Fra Tarkenton botched a pitch-out deep in his own territory an had to fall on the ball in the end zone. The close 2-0 halftim score belied a key difference in the teams; the Pittsburg defense, led by Joe Greene, had successfully shut down Vikin running star Chuck Foreman, while the Steeler offensive lin was opening up constant holes in the Viking front four to allo Franco Harris to go rushing through.

The break that the Steelers were waiting for came on th opening kickoff of the second half, when Minnesota's Bil Brown fumbled the ball and Pittsburgh's Marv Kellum re covered it on the Viking 30-yard line. Harris followed hi offensive line the rest of the way, covering 24 yards in on carry and finally going over for the touchdown on a nine-yar sweep around left end. The 9-0 Steeler lead held up throug the third period, but the Vikings came back with a stron challenge in the final period. A pass interference call on Mik Wagner gave the Vikes the ball on the Steeler five-yard line but Foreman fumbled on the next play and Greene recovere for Pittsburgh. Four plays later, Matt Blair blocked Bobby Walden's punt, with Terry Brown falling on it in the end zone for a Viking touchdown. Fred Cox missed the extra point, and the Steeler defense steadfastly refused to let the Vikes close enough to go for the tying field goal. A 65-yard Pittsburgh drive culminating in a four-yard scoring pass from Terry Bradshaw to Larry Brown iced the game away with 3:31 left.

By the time the final gun sounded the Vikings had their third loss in three attempts, and the Steelers had a host of triumphs which included Franco Harris and his record-setting 158 yards rushing and the happiest owner in pro football in Art Rooney who, after 42 frustrating years, finally claimed his dream—a pro football championship.

SUPER BOWL IX

PITTSBURGH	**0**	**2**	**7**	**7-16**
MINNESOTA	**0**	**0**	**0**	**6- 6**

Second Quarter		
Pitt.	Safety — Tarkenton tackled in end zone	7:49
Third Quarter		
Pitt.	Harris, 12 yard rush PAT — Gerela (kick)	1:35
Fourth Quarter		
Minn.	T. Brown, Recovered blocked punt in end zone Kick failed	4:27
Pitt.	L. Brown, 4 yard pass from Bradshaw PAT — Gerela (kick)	11:29

TEAM STATISTICS

PITT.		MINN.
17	First Downs — Total	9
11	First Downs — Rushing	2
5	First Downs — Passing	5
1	First Downs — Penalty	2
4	Fumbles — Number	3
2	Fumbles — Lost Ball	2
8	Penalties — Number	4
122	Yards Penalized	18
1	Missed Field Goals	1
73	Offensive Plays	47
333	Net Yards	119
4.6	Average Gain	2.5
2	Giveaways	5
5	Takeaways	2
+3	Difference	−3

SUPER BOWL IX

PLAY #1

Francis Tarkenton and the Minnesota Vikings' offensive unit are still trying to get untangled as they mount their first serious drive of the day with the clock winding down in the first half of play. As a result of a safety, (off a poorly executed Tarkenton-to-Osborn handoff), the Vikes are behind, but only by 0-2.

The Steeler defense, especially the front four with All-Pros L. C. Greenwood and Joe Greene on the left, has pretty well bottled up the Viking offense. Some people thought the Steelers would have a real problem containing the mobile Tarkenton. So far, this has not been a problem. In fact, the Vikings have a bigger problem—containing Greenwood. The lanky but quick defensive end seems to have spent the entire first half with a heavily taped hand in Tarkenton's face. Tarkenton has been going to his right most of the day. This is directly at Greene and Greenwood. He's doing this not only with passes, but he's sending his runners in that direction also. Undoubtedly, the Vikings feel this is their point of greatest strength, but it is also a Steeler strong point. While some coaches attack a weakness, others attempt to demoralize an opponent by trying to beat him at his strength. It would seem this has been coach Grant's approach, since a pneumonia-weakened Dwight White is manning the Steelers' right defensive end against Minnesota's left side.

Tark has moved the Vikes from his 35-yard line to the Steelers' 25-yard line. It's now first and 10 with 1:17 left in the half. At this point, Minnesota has many options open in the play-calling department. There's plenty of time to go the 25 yards. Should this not be possible, a Fred Cox field goal would still give the Vikings a 3-2 halftime lead. An additional note: it is unseasonably cold for New Orleans, the wind is gusting in excess of 25 miles per hour, and the field is wet from an early morning rain.

CALL YOUR PLAY:

1. Now is the ideal time to go at White. Call power-sweeps or off-tackle slants with double-team blocking at the defensive left end.

2. Try to surprise the Steeler secondary by trying a some- what out-of-character deep pass on first and 10. Make it a post pattern to John Gilliam.

3. Continue to attempt to establish the running game by going right until it finally works.

4. Let the clock wind down now and kick a field goal—i would be a 42-yarder.

SUPER BOWL IX

PLAY #2

The upstart Steelers are still ahead 9-0, and there are unde 3 minutes to go in the third quarter. Minnesota is still lookin for its offense. Tarkenton is throwing more than running, bu not with that much success. The running game is even les successful—just 11 yards on twelve carries in the first half The main cog in the Vike offense, Chuck Foreman, has no been a factor up to this point. When throwing, Tark still goe mainly to his right.

But after getting the ball at the 20-yard line on Bobby Walde end-zone punt, Minnesota is finally moving. Tark has bee going left, right, and middle with his plays. Nothing, however is going for the big chunks of yardage Minnesota desperatel needs. Despite a bizarre deflected-pass play (Tarkenton t Greenwood back to Tarkenton to Gilliam), which was rule illegal, the Vikes are on the move again, this time at th 47-yard line in Pittsburgh territory.

Two-thirds of the Steeler linebacking corps—All-Pro vetera Andy Russell on the right and Rookie of the Year Jack Lambe in the middle—are out of the game, both leaving with injurie in the first half. This leaves only another All-Pro, Jack Ham of the "originals." Perhaps a real indication of the Steelers' depth and reserve strength is the level of proficiency at which the Steeler defense is still able to function. Of course it helps to have Greene, Greenwood, White, and Ernie Holmes in front of you, but Ed Bradley at middle linebacker and Loren Toews at the outside right are doing more than occupying space or filling out a uniform. Bradley has just dumped Foreman for −2 yards on first down. Toews has made similar contributions since coming on.

Now it is second and 12 for the Vikings at the 47-yard line of the Steelers. How is Tarkenton going to keep the momentum in favor of the Vikings?

CALL YOUR PLAY:

1. Hope to catch Pittsburgh napping and go left with a medium-depth pass.

2. Call a draw, hoping to get Greene and Greenwood penetrating too deeply on the pass rush.

3. Give to Foreman on the same smash at right guard that netted 12 yards recently—the longest run of the day for Minnesota.

4. Have Tarkenton keep around the left side on a keeper rollout.

SUPER BOWL IX

PLAY #3

Ten minutes still remain, and although the Steelers are still dominating the game with their "Steel Curtain" defense, the complexion of the contest is changing. With back-ups Bradley and Toews in regularly on defense, their places on special teams have been taken by others. A missed assignment on the punting team allowed Viking linebacker, Matt Blair, to block Bobby Walden's punt from deep in Steeler territory. It was recovered by Terry Brown in the end zone for a touchdown.

Fred Cox, however, was not successful in his attempt at the point-after. It hit the left upright. This narrowed the gap to 9-6, but any future field goal would only be good for a tie.

Terry Bradshaw, who has directed the Steeler offense faultlessly since taking over in the late season, is doing his best—with a lot of help from his offensive teammates—to change things. Special mention should be made of the work being done by Dan Radakovich's offensive line. Using 8 men interchangeably—Ray Mansfield and Mike Webster at center, Jim Clark, Gerry Mullins, Sam Davis at guards, Mullins, Gordon Gravelle, and Jon Kolb at tackles—the Steelers have not only neutralized the Viking defense, but they've overpowered them. Remember this is a line featuring Alan Page and Doug Sutherland as tackles and Jim Marshall and Carl Eller at the ends.

The Steelers have driven to the Minnesota 4-yard line, the big play being a 30-yard pass to tight end Larry Brown on third and 2. It's third and goal. Franco Harris, who is on his way toward a Super Bowl record of 158 yards rushing, has just picked up 2 yards and lost 1 on the first 2 plays of the series. With the way the defense has been playing, a field goal will help; but one touchdown by Minnesota would hand the young Pittsburgh team a 13-12 loss. Bradshaw needs a touchdown. What will he call? The call will be his, since Chuck Noll gives his quarterback the privilege of calling his own plays on nearly all occasions.

CALL YOUR PLAY:

1. Give to Franco again, hoping for 6 points, but willing to take a short-range field goal.

2. Give to Rocky Bleier, who has broken an early play over right tackle for 17 yards.

3. Have Bradshaw take the snap, fall down, and bring on the field-goal team.

4. Call a rollout to the right with Bradshaw running if it is open or pulling up short and passing to Larry Brown cutting through the end zone.

1975

NFC PLAYOFF 1975

L.A.	**0**	**0**	**0**	**7- 7**
DALLAS	**7**	**14**	**13**	**3-37**

First Quarter

Dall.	P. Pearson, 18 yard pass from Staubach PAT — Fritsch (kick)

Second Quarter

Dall.	Richards, 4 yard pass from Staubach PAT — Fritsch (kick)
Dall.	P. Pearson, 15 yard pass from Staubach PAT — Fritsch (kick)

Third Quarter

Dall.	P. Pearson, 19 yard pass from Staubach PAT — Fritsch (kick)
Dall.	Fritsch, 40 yard field goal
Dall.	Fritsch, 26 yard field goal

Fourth Quarter

L.A.	Cappelletti, 1 yard rush PAT — Dempsey (kick)
Dall.	Fritsch, 26 yard field goal

TEAM STATISTICS

L.A.		DALL
9	First Downs — Total	24
1	First Downs — Rushing	8
7	First Downs — Passing	15
1	First Downs — Penalty	1
1	Fumbles — Number	1
0	Fumbles — Lost Ball	0
4	Penalties — Number	5
25	Yards Penalized	59
2	Missed Field Goals	0
45	Offensive Plays	78
118	Net Yards	441
2.6	Average Gain	5.[illegible]
3	Giveaways	1
1	Takeaways	3
−2	Difference	+2

NFC PLAYOFF 1975

PLAY #1

Not all Monday morning quarterbacks have to wait until Monday to do their quarterbacking. In some situations he can assume his leadership role on Sunday. Such is the case in this game.

Chuck Knox has done an outstanding job since coming to Los Angeles. He has had his team in the playoffs each season, and although he's not taken them to a Super Bowl, he's generally regarded as being in the upper echelon of NFC coaches. Today, however, he's got a tough decision to make—one that will leave him open to second-guessing.

Quarterback James Harris is hurting. Harris looked so good during the 1974 season that Knox traded John Hadl to Green Bay in midseason. All Harris did was lead the Rams into the NFC final against the Minnesota Vikings. However, Harris's shoulder isn't 100 percent, and Knox has used young Ron Jaworski at quarterback of late. All Jaworski did in this third year out of Youngstown State, was beat the defending world champion Pittsburgh Steelers on the last Saturday of the season and direct the win over the explosive St. Louis Cardinals in the first round of the playoffs. Harris thought himself ready for that game, but Knox stuck with the youngster. Harris didn't say much after the Ram win. He didn't stick around the locker room that long, but he was obviously disappointed with the head coach's decision on quarterbacking.

While praising young Jaworski, Knox was quoted as saying, "Harris is still our number one quarterback." Was he, after all? Is he? What about "The Polish Rifle?" How do the players feel about it in this big game. Did Knox learn anything in the pregame warm-ups? Did the Cowboys?

CALL YOUR PLAY:

1. Start Harris, but be ready to go to Jaworski.

2. Start Jaworski, but be ready to go to Harris.

3. Send out an SOS for Bob Waterfield.

4. Find Karl Sweetan, or maybe it would be better to find the guy Sweetan tried to interest in that Ram play-book.

NFC PLAYOFF 1975

PLAY #2

Considering the circumstances surrounding the game and the way things are happening on the field, the Rams must be given credit for hanging in. They're only down by an 0-7 count at this time, which isn't bad for a team whose offense is nearly nonexistent so far. Here's what the offense has done: first series, punt on fourth and 15; second series, intercepted on second down; third series, punt on fourth and 8; fourth series, on fourth and 7 a field-goal attempt from the 34-yard line blocked. But as the first period is ending, Ron Jaworski, on a drive that began at his 32-yard line, is moving the Rams' offense. The quarter ends in the middle of the drive with the Rams at the Dallas 47-yard line, first and 10.

Jaworski, mixing his plays like a 12-year veteran, resumes the drive and has the Rams rolling. The youngster has overcome several obstacles in the drive already. He's been sacked by Harvey Banks Martin (and that's about as sacked as you can get). This lost 12 yards. An illegal procedure penalty gave him third and 15 instead of third and 10. Nevertheless, he's picked up 14 of the 15 needed yards and is now facing a fourth and 1. The ball is at the Dallas 24-yard line.

It goes without saying that the Rams must do something here. It's early in the game, but sideline observers will tell you that they are missing the "fire" of a championship team at this time. How do they shake themselves up? Go for it?

Time isn't a factor, but psychologically, Knox's club is in a critical situation. Would a field goal give them enough of a boost? Twice in this drive Jaworski has hit wide receiver Ron Jessie for good yardage. He's also gotten 7 yards himself on a keeper. Lawrence McCutcheon hasn't run that well, but he's turned a swing pass into a 14-yard gain.

CALL YOUR PLAY:

1. Get some points! Have Tom Dempsey kick a 41-yard field goal.

2. Have Jaworski take it on a keeper around the right side.

3. Throw a look-in to Jessie.

4. Punt to the "coffin corner."

NFC PLAYOFF 1975

PLAY #3

Dallas is taking advantage of everything the Rams are giving them. Midway into the second quarter, they are owners of a 14-0 lead. Roger Staubach, going into the recently revived "shotgun" formation on occasion, is mixing passes with runs and pretty much playing his game.

Taking over on the 33-yard line, Staubach begins driving the Cowboy offense. He's putting together a drive that resembles something he'd do in a dummy scrimmage. Passing and running, he moves the ball club from his 33-yard line to the Rams' 15 with only one third-down situation—a third and 3, on which he keeps around his right end for 9 yards. Now with 1:21 left in the period, he's faced with a third and 1 at the Ram 15-yard line.

With the luxury of a 14-0 lead, Roger Dodger can do just about what he wants, provided his wants coincide with those of Dallas head coach Tom Landry. What will Landry send in? A basic running play? A pass? Something that will leave a shot at a field goal if the selected third-down play should not get the yardage necessary to convert? Staubach has had so much success up to now that almost any play would seem to have a good chance to being successful. Doug Dennison, from Kutztown State (the same school that produced Jim Youngman), Preston Pearson, Robert Newhouse, and Staubach himself have all been very effective running with the ball. Staubach is also 7 completions in 14 attempts in the passing category. Another factor to weigh: a Toni Fritsch field goal, if needed, would be from no farther out than the 32-yard line. How will the Rams' defense deploy and what will they look for?

CALL YOUR PLAY:

1. Send Staubach on a rollout right, keeping.

2. Send Staubach on a rollout right, passing to Newhouse, who has faked through the line.

3. Try a deep pass to Preston Pearson coming out of the backfield, figuring field goal on fourth and 1 if the pass is unsuccessful.

4. Newhouse up the middle, where he's had some success.

AFC PLAYOFF 1975

PITT.	**0**	**0**	**0**	**7- 7**
DALLAS	**7**	**14**	**13**	**3-37**

Second Quarter

Pit.	Gerela, 36 yard field goal

Fourth Quarter

Pit.	Harris, 25 yard rush PAT — Gerela (kick)
Oak.	Siani, 14 yard pass from Stabler PAT — Blanda (kick)
Pit.	Stallworth, 20 yard pass from Bradshaw PAT — Kick No Good
Oak.	Blanda, 41 yard field goal

TEAM STATISTICS

PIT.		**OAK.**
16	First Downs — Total	18
5	First Downs — Rushing	3
10	First Downs — Passing	13
1	First Downs — Penalty	2
5	Fumbles — Number	4
5	Fumbles — Lost Ball	3
3	Penalties — Number	4
32	Yards Penalized	40
2	Missed Field Goals	1
64	Offensive Plays	76
332	Net Yards	321
5.2	Average Gain	4.2
8	Giveaways	5
5	Takeaways	8
−3	Difference	+3

AFC PLAYOFF 1975

PLAY #1

This classic-to-be never really turned out that way. The Pittsburgh weather bureau delivered a frozen field and 16 degrees for the game. And any thoughts of a typical Steeler-Raider classic were soon banished. It was a classic only in the sense of the tremendous hitting demonstrated by both defenses. Otherwise it was a weather-aided production of fumbles, dropped passes, intercepted passes, slips and slides, and anything else that could go wrong.

The first quarter was scoreless, but with just over 7 minutes left in the second period, the Steelers broke the ice (pun intended) on Roy Gerela's 36-yard field goal. The 3-0 score stood at the end of the half. Statistically, Oakland had a slight edge in total offense—147 yards to 132. They also had the ball more—41 plays to 27. Terry Bradshawa was intercepted 3 times, Ken Stabler only once; but Bradshaw had 105 yards passing, while Stabler managed 77. The Steeler running game of Franco Harris and Rocky Bleier wasn't in gear yet. They gained only 27 yards, with Franco's 7-yarder the long one.

The same lonely 3 points were still the total scoring output as the fourth quarter began, and Pittsburgh fans were beginning to envision a repetition of 1972, when two Gerela field goals were the only scores until Stabler "snaked" around left end on a 30-yard scramble to give the Raiders a 7-6 lead with [illegible] minutes remaining in the game (the game ended 13-7 on Franco's "Immaculate Reception").

But on the first play of the last period, Franco cracks left end, shakes off Neal Colzie, and dashes into the end zone 25 yards away. Oakland followed with a quick, retaliatory touchdown, Stabler passing to tight end Dave Casper 3 straight times for 56 yards and then finding Mike Siani in the end zone with a 14 yard strike—making it 10-7, Steelers. However, a Marv Hubbard fumble is recovered by Jack Lambert (his third recovery of the day) at the Oakland 25-yard line. Two charges by Franco at the middle of the Raider defense net 5 yards. Now it's third and 5 from the 20-yard line.

CALL YOUR PLAY:

1. Continue to bang away with Franco, controlling the ball and the clock. Run him off right tackle.

2. Strike quickly on a flag route to wide receiver Johnny Stallworth in the left corner of the end zone.

3. Rollout with Bradshaw running right.

4. Try for field position and take a field goal if needed.

AFC PLAYOFF 1975

PLAY #2

The Steelers kick off with over 9 minutes left, and for several series hold the Raiders. Now they are driving toward the score that could nail the lid on the Raiders' coffin. But Franco Harris fumbles as he hits over left guard, and Ted Hendricks recovers. Hendricks, pressed into service in an odd 3-4 defense (3 linemen and 4 linebackers) against Cincinnati last week, tore the Bengals apart. He's not been a factor thus far today, but his recovery gives the ball to Oakland at the Raider 35-yard line with 1:31 remaining on the clock.

Since they need at least a touchdown and a field goal, Kenny Stabler is passing on all downs. He's hitting too. An 8-yarder to Siani gives Oakland a second and 2 at the Steeler 32-yard line, but the last time-out has been taken on the play. There are 24 seconds remaining. Stabler looks for and throws to Morris Bradshaw in the end zone. Incomplete.

Now the strategy board goes to work. How will they attempt to get a field goal, a touchdown, and a PAT squeezed into 24 seconds? Somewhere an onside kick will probably figure into it, but let's take one step at a time. Since they need the field goal anyway, would it be better to take it now, try the onside kick (hopefully recover), and then go for the touchdown?

This would seem logical; but the kick would be a 41-yarder by the 48-year-old George Blanda, and he's already missed from 38 yards out with a lot less pressure on him than now. Another pass into the end zone would only use a few seconds, and then they'd need only a field goal—assuming a touchdown on the pass and recovery of the onside kick. What will the Raider choice be?

CALL YOUR PLAY:

1. Kick the field goal now, even though it is just third down.

2. Try an end-zone pass to Cliff Branch, working against Mel Blount.

3. Try a sideline pattern to tight end Dave Casper for a closer field goal.

4. Try a run for a first down. It would stop the clock to move the chains, and shorten the field-goal yardage—especially if it got more than the 2 yards needed.

AFC PLAYOFF 1975

PLAY #3

As the Raiders line up to kick off with 12 seconds left in the game, everyone knew an outside kick was coming. The only element of suspense was: where would Oakland kick the ball? As it turned out, they kicked to Johnny Stallworth. His hands, which had hauled in the earlier touchdown, betrayed him now, and he couldn't control the ball. There was a swarming, swirling pile-up, and it was Raider Marv Hubbard who made the recovery at the Raider 48-yard line.

This took 5 seconds. Now Ken Stabler had 7 seconds to work some magic. There are no time-outs, remember. How many times can he pass in 7 seconds? If it's more than once, chances are that they'd be too short. It would take quickly thrown passes, and they wouldn't be likely to produce the yardage needed. Will he go for broke with one last pass? If not, he'll have to use the sidelines, and there lie some of the iciest parts of a bad field which has gotten worse. Knowing that Stabler must throw deep and quickly, the Steelers are in a "prevent" defense. They will give up almost anything except a touchdown, since a field goal would still leave the scoreboard reading Pittsburgh 16 and Oakland 13. Stabler knows exactly what has to be done, and his past performances prove that he can move a team to a score with no time-outs better than almost anyone. Adding to the confusion, fans have poured out of the stands and are now ringing the field right up to the 3-foot sideline mark. Will Stabler be able to pull off one more miracle? Remember the Oakland-Miami playoff game of 1974? As he was going down to his knees (literally), Stabler got off a pass to Clarence Davis for a touchdown in that one, and stranger things have happened in other Raider-Steeler games.

CALL YOUR PLAY:

1. Flood the end zone with all eligible receivers and hope to find one open.

2. Throw to Cliff Branch in the end zone on a fly or up pattern.

3. Call a draw play to Clarence Davis and hope the unorthodox call and his speed can get him into the end zone. A touchdown on the running play would use the remaining time.

4. Throw deep to Branch as he angles toward the sideline. This would allow him to get out of bounds or, if open, to turn on the after-burners and sprint to end zone.

Swann's Song

SUPER BOWL X

January 18, at Miami
(Attendance 80,187)

Unlike past Super Bowl efforts, which had more fanfare off the field than on, this year's edition featured enough excitement to compete with the pre-game show. Favorite Pittsburgh, returning for the second time in two years, was facing Dallas, the first wildcard team to ever reach the NFL finals.

Through the first three quarters Dallas held a 10-7 lead. Then, at 3:32 of the final quarter, Reggie Harrison, a Pittsburgh reserve running back who plays on special teams, blocked a punt by Mitch Hoopes at the Dallas 9. The ball bounced off Harrison's face hard enough to wind up in the Dallas end zone, good enough for a two-point safety and run the score to 10-9. It was a play which was considered the turning point of the game. Roy Gerela put Pittsburgh in front for the first time with a 36-yard field at 6:19. A few minutes later Mike Wagner intercepted a Roger Staubach pass and returned it 19 yards to the Dallas 7. Terry Bradshaw was unable to get the touchdown, but Gerela booted an 18-yard field goal.

With the score 15-10, the game's hero, Lynn Swann, took a 59-yard pass from Bradshaw and ran it 5 yards into the end zone at 11:58. The kick failed and the stage was set for the final dramatics. The Cowboys drove 80 yards in five plays with under two minutes to play to make the score 21-17. On the drive, two passes of 30 and 11 yards from Staubach to Drew Pearson proved the key. Terry Hanratty replacing Bradshaw, who had been shaken up on his 64-yard pass to Swann, for Pittsburgh's last offensive series and found himself with fourth down and 9 to go on the Dallas 41. Only 1:28 was left to play and coach Chuck Noll decided to gamble, owing to the fact that Dallas had no time outs left. Rather than punt and risk the run back, he had the Steelers go for the run. They got two yards and Dallas took possession. Five plays later the game was over and Pittsburgh had its second straight Super Bowl triumph.

Dallas coach Tom Landry blamed the defeat on the blocked punt by Harrison, which he said changed the momentum of the game around. He may have been right, but Swann's performance—which earned him the game's Most Valuable Player ward—was momentum enough for the Steelers. Hospitalized nly two weeks earlier with a concussion, and dropping passes ı practice, the fleet-footed receiver returned to catch four asses for an astonishing total of 161 yards—a Super Bowl ecord certain to stand for many years.

SUPER BOWL X

PITT.	**7**	**0**	**0**	**14-21**
DALLAS	**7**	**3**	**0**	**7-17**

rst Quarter

Dall.	D. Pearson, 29 yard pass from Staubach PAT — Fritsch (kick)	4:36
Pitt.	Grossman, 7 yard pass from Bradshaw PAT — Gerela (kick)	9:03

econd Quarter

Dall.	Fritsch, 36 yard field goal	0:15

urth Quarter

Pitt.	Safety — Harrison blocked punt out of end zone	3:32
Pitt.	Gerela, 36 yard field goal	6:19
Pitt.	Gerela, 18 yard field goal	8:23
Pitt.	Swann, 64 yard pass from Bradshaw PAT — Gerela (kick failed)	11:58
Dall.	P. Howard, 34 yard pass from Staubach PAT — Fritsch (kick)	13:12

'it.	TEAM STATISTICS	Dall.
3	First Downs — Total	14
7	First Downs — Rushing	6
6	First Downs — Passing	8
0	First Downs — Penalty	0
4	Fumbles — Number	4
0	Fumbles — Lost Ball	0
0	Penalties — Number	2
0	Yards Penalized	20
2	Missed Field Goals	0
7	Offensive Plays	62
9	Net Yards	270
5.1	Average Gain	4.4
0	Giveaways	3
3	Takeaways	0
3	Difference	−3

SUPER BOWL X

PLAY #1

A fired-up Dallas team is ahead 7-0 with less than 5 minute gone in the game as a result of a bobbled snap on a punt followed by a lightning-quick touchdown pass from Roge Staubach to Drew Pearson. But Pittsburgh is now drivin steadily toward the Dallas goal and a "get-even" touchdown Seven plays have put the Steelers on the Dallas 7-yard lin in a third and 1 situation. With the exception of a second-dow 32-yard pass to Lynn Swann, quarterback Terry Bradsha has been letting running backs Franco Harris and Rock Bleier "do their thing," with able assistance from a cohesiv offensive line.

As has been the case all season long in short-yardage situa tions, coach Chuck Noll has "overloaded" the offensiv formation with blockers. Larry Brown, the regular tight end is in his normal position. He is joined by second-year ma Randy Grossman as a second tight end. Gerry Mullins, starting guard who has caught several touchdowns when use as a second tight end, is also in. This time he is set to the righ of the basic formation as a wingback. The normal guard spo is taken by Sam Davis. While Mullins is primarily a blocke he can legally be thrown to.

The Dallas defense is dug in. Their first responsibility i to shut off the run. But with all those tight ends running around they should also be thinking pass. Perhaps they should ke on Mullins. In the past he has simply started in motion bac toward the center of the formation and ploughed into the are where a running back has been given a handoff. This create tremendous blocking power at the point of attack, and ha usually given the back the necessary crack he needs to ge whatever yardage is required on the play.

CALL YOUR PLAY:

1. Cut down on the ball-handling, follow wedge blocking in the middle, and have Bradshaw sneak for the yard. As powerful as he is, he may also get you the touchdown.

2. Put Mullins in motion back toward the ball for additional blocking and give to Franco, "the second man through." He'll follow the lead block by Bleier, who is sometimes described as "the Steelers' third guard."

3. Use a play-action call, with Mullins coming back toward the center as he usually does—starting in motion before the snap. Have Bradshaw roll out right and toss to Grossman "squaring out" in the end zone.

4. Have Mullins slip out into the flat and take a pass from Bradshaw.

SUPER BOWL X

PLAY #2

Dallas is now ahead 10-7 as a result of a 36-yard field goal by former Austrian soccer star Toni Fritsch. The field goal was the finishing play of a well-mixed drive to the Steeler 14-yard line.

Pittsburgh is mounting a drive following the kickoff, with Bradshaw running Franco Harris and Rocky Bleier, and using second-year wide receiver Johnny Stallworth. Stallworth has caught two balls and barely missed a Bradshaw overthrow in this series. The Steelers are looking at a fourth and 2 on the 36-yard line of Dallas. Franco has just been stopped cold by Harvey Banks Martin on third and 2.

It's very early in the second quarter, but the defending Super Bowl champions find themselves behind to a young team they expected to have under control. Is it a good time to gamble on fourth down? It would be great if it works, but if the opportunistic young Dallas club were to hold the world champs, it would give them even more momentum. From the Steeler point of view, the temptation to gamble has to be considerable. A successful conversion on fourth down, especially if it were to lead to a touchdown, would mean a lot to the Steeler cause. It would put them right back in the game and at the same time give the Cowboys something to think about.

If the Steelers do gamble, what type of play will they use. Would they again go to the "overloaded" formation that resulted in Grossman's touchdown? Would they simply snap the ball to the man—Frenchy Fuqua—blocking in punt formation? Or would they have Bobby Walden run or pass out of the deep position? All this may be academic if Pittsburgh just punts away.

CALL YOUR PLAY:

1. Punt with no attempt at any type of fake.

2. Attempt a long field goal. It would be a 53-yard attempt, and Roy Gerela's kicking seems to be somewhat weaker since he bruised his ribs making the tackle on the Cowboys' deep-reverse kickoff return.

3. Use the short-yardage set, and have Franco hit off tackle on a slant. Try the right side.

4. Use the short-yardage set, but instead of running or passing to Grossman, throw to Franco swinging to the right out of the backfield.

SUPER BOWL X

PLAY #3

Switching from the role of the intimidated to the intimidators, the Steelers, at one point, seemed to be in control of the game. But a series of events finds the Pittsburgh lead cut to just 4 points at 21-17. In addition, quarterback Terry Bradshaw has been injured; earlier in the game, as he threw a touchdown "bomb" to antelope wide receiver Lynn Swann, Bradshaw fell victim to a "blitz" by Dallas strong safety Cliff Harris

Dallas's Toni Fritsch attempts a short, onside kick, and aking the recovery for Pittsburgh is offensive lineman Gerry ullins. The Steelers take over on the Dallas 42-yard line ith Terry Hanratty now at quarterback. Franco Harris loses d then gains 2 yards on the first two downs. On third and Rocky Bleier is sent over left guard. He gains a yard. Now is fourth down, and 9 yards are needed to keep the drive ve. More logically, it is time to punt.

With the clock showing 1:28 left in the game, there is still ne for the Cowboys, more particularly Roger Staubach, to rk some of the lightning that struck the Minnesota Vikings dramatically in the playoffs. But Staubach will be somewhat ndicapped (should Dallas get the ball) in that Dallas has ed all of their time-outs. Hanratty's previous three plays the series represent virtually all of his playing time this ason. The 7-year veteran has not attempted a pass all season ng. On occasion, the Cowboys have mounted a substantial ss rush, and Dallas has also taken away the effectiveness Franco (and Bleier) for the moment. Punting out of danger ay not be as easy as it would seem. Bobby Walden bobbled e snap early in the game, giving Dallas excellent field sition, and the Cowboy "bomb-squadders" have come se on several punts and field-goal attempts.

ALL YOUR PLAY:

1. Huddle with the punting team on the sideline and make rtain everyone is 100 percent ready and very certain on the ocking assignments. Then punt away as deeply as possible, ll allowing for maximum coverage.

2. Same as above, but instruct Walden to angle deep and t of bounds, thus eliminating any kind of runback.

3. Try a relatively safe pass—for example, a screen or a re to one of the running backs.

4. Call a running play with a minimum of ball-handling. ne designed to use as much time as possible, rather than one signed for a first down.

Answers

FL PLAYOFF 1966 — PLAY #1

Meredith went long to Clarke. Clarke went even longer imself. The big flanker, who also plays some tight end, took e pass at midfield and turned it into a 68-yard touchdown ıss. The PAT put the Cowboys just 7 points back.

FL PLAYOFF 1966 — PLAY #2

Meredith rolled to his right. Dave Robinson was on Meredith xtremely quickly, and the lanky Dallas signal-caller was orced to sidearm a desperation pass. It fluttered into the end one, but considering the pressure exerted by Robinson, leredith was to be commended for even getting it off. Tom rown made up for earlier mistakes by picking off the ball the end zone. Two plays later (Starr simply flopped on the all twice) the game was over.

FL PLAYOFF 1966 — PLAY #1

Dawson went all out on the play. Arbanas took off down e field, running a deep flag route and brought in Dawson's row in the end zone. It gave the Chiefs an early 7-0 lead nd took full advantage of an early break.

FL PLAYOFF 1966 — PLAY #2

Kemp threw toward Bobby Crockett (like Burnett, a oungster out of Arkansas). It seemed like a good call, specially as Kansas City cornerback Willie Mitchell slipped the "goo." However, free safety Johnny Robinson crossed ver to make the interception at the goal line. He took it back 2 yards to the Buffalo 28-yard line. With :03 on the clock, Iike Mercer toed a 32-yard field goal, and instead of being ed at 14-14, Buffalo was down 17-7.

UPER BOWL I — PLAY #1

Starr, if anything, is predictable in that he is unpredictable. his third-and-one situation is tailor-made for him. Even if

Kansas City suspects that he will go "long," they don't kno how or where it will occur. Starr called a play-action pass t McGee. The running-play fake to Jimmy Taylor froze th Kansas City defense temporarily, if it didn't completely fo them. This gave McGee the time he needed to break fro Mitchell's coverage. The 34-year-old split end made a bac bending, juggling catch at the Chief 19, having gotten positio on Mitchell, and out-distanced all Kansas City defenders ov the goal. This gave Green Bay the first score and set th tempo of the game to a great extent. McGee, who only caug four passes all year as a part-time player, would have "th best day he's had in ten years," to quote Chief wide receiv Chris Burford from a postgame interview.

SUPER BOWL I — PLAY #2

Starr again called the play-action with a deep pass to receiver open in the confused Chiefs' secondary. This time was Carroll Dale, who caught the ball at the Kansas Ci 33-yard line and sprinted into the end zone with no one clos to him. The play covered 64 yards; however, it was no goo An unidentified Green Bay interior lineman had moved aft being in a set position. The subsequent penalty nullifed th long-distance reception and score. This only delayed th inevitable. On third and 6 (a result of the 5-yard penalty f illegal procedure), Green Bay made 10 yards when Starr four McGee open on a post pattern to keep the drive alive. It to ten plays, but Taylor got the touchdown on the fabled Gree Bay power-sweep around his left end from 14 yards ou Although Taylor got blocking from Bob Skoronski, Fre "Fuzzy" Thurston, and Jerry Kramer pulling, he, himse ran right over several Chiefs.

SUPER BOWL I — PLAY #3

Dawson went with a relatively safe call. He used play-actio faking a run, pulling out, and passing toward Arbanas. Ho ever, Bengtson had changed defensive tactics at halftim He was so sure that Dawson would not use the run, but alwa pass after faking, that he had his superb linebacking corps middleman Ray Nitschke and outside backers Lee Roy Caff and Dave Robinson just ignore the fake run and play the pas

In addition, he also had them "red-dog" or "blitz." This added to the pressure the front four was putting on Dawson. So intense was the heat on Dawson that his pass fluttered toward Arbanas instead of zipping. All-Pro free safety Willie Wood simply stepped in front of the big tight end and made the interception, which he returned to the Chiefs' 5-yard line. Pitts scored for Green Bay on the next play.

NFL PLAYOFF 1967 — PLAY #1

During their careers certain players conjure up certain images merely with the mention of their name. Say "Bart Starr," and immediately anyone knowing anything about pro football, especially prematurely retired defensive backs, sees the Green Bay quarterback in a "third and short" call, pulling the ball away from a faking back and lofting it to a streaking wide receiver. Starr went on record early as indicating that a little nip in the air wasn't going to force him from his game. He called a play-action pass, first faking to Ben Wilson, and then tossing deep to Boyd Dowler near the goal line. Dowler made the catch, having shaken off the coverage of Mel Renfro. Candidly, it should be pointed out that the pass looked to be overthrown, but a friendly Green Bay breeze caused the ball to hang long enough for the 6'5" receiver to make the grab.

NFL PLAYOFF 1967 — PLAY #2

The call was an option pass, but Reeves disguised it very well. So well that it resembled a sweep that had worked in an earlier situation. Packer All-Pro safety, Willie Wood, reacted to a run. As he did this, Reeves pulled up and threw deep to Lance Rentzel. The swift, young receiver breezed right by Bob Jeter, who had no help from Wood, and took the pass far downfield. He raced into the end zone as the Cowboys went into the lead for the first time.

NFL PLAYOFF 1967 — PLAY #3

If you were following pro football then, you know that Lombardi and Starr settled on the there's-no-tomorrow quarterback sneak. It worked! Starr said the call gave him a shorter distance to run and eliminated the need for a handoff. He ran to his right, just off the center, because Jerry Kramer was having a better time of it with Jethro Pugh than young Gale Gillingham was with Bob Lilly. Also Kramer lined up on a spot that afforded him better traction and footing. Pugh cooperated unintentionally by lining up on Kramer's inside shoulder. This gave the All-Pro guard a good blocking angle. At the snap, Kramer fired out at Pugh and moved him back. Starr burrowed into the end zone as Mercein came flying into him to give added impetus. While the newly devised concept of instant replay launched Kramer's literary career, it should be pointed out that Kramer received an able assist from center Ken Bowman in blocking out Pugh.

AFL PLAYOFF 1967 — PLAY #1

Calling a sweep-left aimed at Houston's right side, Lamonica pitched out to Hewritt Dixon, and the play was run perfectly. Dixon got a crunching block from Upshaw, and when the dust cleared, he was 69 yards downfield in the end zone for the first touchdown of the day.

SUPER BOWL II — PLAY #1

Given the green light by Coach Lombardi on fourth and 1 (actually it's more a foot than a yard for the first), Starr hands off to big Ben Wilson on the sweep to the left side. The play is led by the left tackle, Bob Skoronski, the young left guard, Gale Gillingham, and a pulling right guard, All-Timer Jerry Kramer. Also getting into the flow of the play is the other Green Bay set-back, Donny Anderson. This convoy cuts the effectiveness of the Oakland defense so much so that Wilson gets the needed yard and 4 more to spare before he is downed by Raider cornerback Howie Williams. The quarter ends, but the drive continues. However, sacks of Starr by Keating and Birdwell leave the Pack with too much yardage to make up, and they take a 20-yard Chandler kick for 3 points and a 6-0 lead in the game.

SUPER BOWL II — PLAY #2

Starr's well-earned reputation as an unorthodox play-caller gained added stature as he dropped back and threw long to his 6'5'' flankerback Dowler. Oakland cornerbacks Kent

IcCloughan and Willie Brown are very adept at the AFL bump and run'' pass defense: the cornerbacks play closer the receivers as they leave the line of scrimmage and stay ith them stride for stride, jostling them as they run their atterns. This knocks the receivers off stride and breaks up e timing between quarterback and receiver. Dowler, how- 'er, had found a way of combatting it. McCloughan bumped m, but Dowler was the one to do the running—right past IcCloughan—taking Starr's pass in stride at midfield and oing unmolested the remaining yards. The 62-yard strike ade it 13-0, after Chandler's extra point.

UPER BOWL II — PLAY #3

To the surprise of nearly no one, with the possible exception f the Oakland Raider secondary, Starr did go to his old buddy IcGee. Max turned it into a 35-yard gain. Illustrating the dvantage of working with someone with whom you are very amiliar, Starr saw the Oakland defender react to McGee and rew to Max's side, away from the cornerback; McGee eached back and made the reception. All this was done without IcGee having to detour from his basic pass route. From the akland 25-yard line, the Pack continued to drive toward the aider goal. Donny Anderson cracked over the goal from the -yard line for the eventual touchdown, which made it 23-7, ackers up. After the game, McGee's last ever, he told of okingly asking Dowler to get hurt, "so I can catch one more."

FL PLAYOFF 1968 — PLAY #1

Not having the benefit of knowing what was to follow, the olts took the field-goal attempt, and Michaels made it good om 28 yards out. It was just the beginning. Matte would et three touchdowns and Timmy Brown would add another.

FL PLAYOFF 1968 — PLAY #1

Namath called for more lightning. This was the third time struck in one spot—Shea Stadium. Mathis was brought in, nd the original call was a swing pass to him in the right corner the end zone. He was covered, so Namath, given good otection by a revamped Jet offensive line, swung around his left and drilled a "frozen rope" to Maynard in the nd zone. It was pure Namath, the Namath that a great quarterbacking legend was built upon—an 80-yard drive • three plays in 31 seconds.

AFL PLAYOFF 1968 — PLAY #2

The play called was a pass to Biletnikoff. Whether or n he was open and could have caught the ball is purely academi Huge Verlon Biggs, the Jets' defensive end, took care of tha He stormed through the Raiders' protective cup and dropp Lamonica before he had time to throw. The Jets had the ba (and appeared to have the game) at their 34-yard line. A they had to do was run out the clock.

AFL PLAYOFF 1968 — PLAY #3

Lamonica had every intention of throwing to Biletniko but he was not open. Neither were the other two men downfiel Charlie Smith, sensing this, sneaked out to the right in t swing-pass area. Daryle threw to him, but it was costly. T toss was incomplete, but what the rookie running back did realize was that the ball was not a forward pass, but actual tossed backward and fully recoverable as a lateral. Lamoni later said, "I realized this right away, but Baker (Jet lineback Ralph Baker, who made the recovery and took it far downfiel got to the ball ahead of me."

Hindsight, which is always 20/20, gives a perfect look how much better a field goal would have been earlier on th infamous fourth and 10, but who's to say it would have be good? Who's to say the Raiders would have been back at t Jets' 24-yard line?

SUPER BOWL III — PLAY #1

Morrall's call was the pass to Mitchell, and it seems to ha been a good one; but Middle linebacker Al Atkinson of t Jets fully extended himself and made a leaping tip of the pa This caused the ball to change direction slightly, and inste of hitting Mitchell in the hands, the pass hit his shoulder p as he twisted himself back for the ball. The carom was field by Jet right cornerback Randy Beverly—more because he w faked out of position by Mitchell on his pass route than any ball-hawking abilities he might have possessed. A touc back was the result, along with 0 Colt points—again. T subsequent drive by Namath, one in which he mixed passes well with runs at the Baltimore right defensive flank (manned by aging Don Shinnick and Ordell Braase), resulted in the Jets breaking the scoring ice to take a 7-0 lead.

SUPER BOWL III — PLAY #2

The call by Shula during the sideline huddle with Morrall was the "flea-flicker." It developed beautifully. Morrall "had time to read the Sunday comics" (as writers used to say), after taking Matte's pitch-back. Jimmy Orr was free of any Jet defensive back and was roaming the end zone, "wig-wagging" for Morrall to throw to him. However, with so many Colt potential receivers out into patterns and Jets' defenders dropping back also, Morrall's line of vision to Orr was obscured. Despite Orr's desperate signaling, Morrall didn't locate him. He turned instead to Jerry Hill. He tossed toward Hill at the Jet 12-yard line—not a bad place to be. But Jet strong safety Jim Hudson was also there, and it was he who claimed the pass. Time ran out and still it was New York 7 and Baltimore 0.

SUPER BOWL III — PLAY #3

The Colts went for the onside kick even though the element of surprise was missing. Nevertheless, tight end Tom Mitchell gained possession of the kick for the Colts. They got the ball at the Jets' 44-yard line. Unitas alternated strikes to Richardson and Orr, but at the 19-yard line three straight incompletions all but finished the Colts, even though 2:21 remained. The Colts got another possession, at their own 34-yard line, but only 8 seconds remained in a game that would be described as "the best thing to happen to pro football."

NFL PLAYOFF 1969 — PLAY #1

Kapp throws deep. Not with much style, but with a lot of effect. At midfield, Washington takes the pass and continues on downfield for the 75-yard touchdown. Cox's second PAT makes it 14-0, and there is still most of the first quarter left to play.

AFL PLAYOFF 1969 — PLAY #1

The field goal was the call and it was good. The lead now jumped to 10 points. Dawson later fumbled—the Chiefs lost four out of five miscues—at his own 13-yard line. But because of the successful Stenerud field goal, the Raiders felt a field goal of their own was not worth that much, and the drive fizzled without any Raider points.

SUPER BOWL IV — PLAY #1

Innovative Hank Stram called for the Stenerud field-goal attempt. It was good. The 3 points helped, but there was an unseen "bonus" that was to aid the cause of the AFL club later in the game. The Chiefs made it emphatically clear in the early going that they weren't to be intimidated by the Vikings. Even if Stenerud had missed, the idea of the Chiefs being a scoring threat anytime they crossed the center of the field had to have an adverse effect on the Minnesota club. In candid reactions after the game, more than one Viking readily admitted this when questioned about it. Stenerud's kick, which was good with a considerable amount to spare, was all that Kansas City got in the first period, but it was 3 points more than what Minnesota had registered.

SUPER BOWL IV — PLAY #2

Cool and calculating Bud Grant, as conservative in his first Super Bowl appearance as he would be in subsequent games, declined to match wits with Hank Stram, or at least declined to match the toe of Fred Cox with that of Jan Stenerud. Grant's decision was to have Bob Lee punt away. This Lee did, although as the third-string quarterback, he would have been an excellent choice to pass from punt formation. Lee's punt went into the end zone for a touchback, and Dawson took over at the 20-yard line. The drive which ensued resulted in another Jan Stenerud field goal and a 6-0 lead for a team that was to pay the price for what the Jets had done a year earlier to the NFL's Colts.

SUPER BOWL IV — PLAY #3

The 51 G-O reverse from the tight "I" was the call. It turned out to be a good one too, not to mention daring. It was the third time in the game that Stram sent the particular play in, and the third time that it worked to near perfection. Each time the play was called, the Kansas City club was in a crucial situation. Each time, Pitts made the necessary yardage with little to spare, but he made it.

On this third-and-7 play, the key factor was Carl Eller's quick reaction to the fakes going left. He was caught inside and sealed off and Pitts sped around his vacated flank. Mackbee made the stop after about a 7-yard run, but Pitts and the Chiefs had converted a critical third-down play. This enabled the Chiefs to keep the drive alive, and two plays later Dawson hit Otis Taylor on a little "hitch" pattern in front of Mackbee. It was a 6-yard pass, but the talented Taylor broke two Minnesota tackles, literally, and broke Minnesota's backs, figuratively, on a 46-yard touchdown run, making the score 23-7. It would end that way.

NFC PLAYOFF 1970 — PLAY #1

Dallas coach Tom Landry, despite the condition of Morton's arm, sends in the play-action pass to Garrison with a fake handoff to Thomas. It works to perfection, thanks especially to Thomas's fake into the line. This score enables the Cowboys to withstand a later John Brodie touchdown pass and a fourth-quarter rally.

AFC PLAYOFF 1970 — PLAY #1

Seriously, sports fans, the call was the Statue of Liberty. Bulaich took the ball from Unitas and raced around left end for the touchdown. The big assist on the play was a double-duty block thrown by Nowatzke. It got Ben Davidson AND Gus Otto.

AFC PLAYOFF 1970 — PLAY #2

Unitas made the call. In Colt terminology, it's a "double-bow out." Translated into laymen's terms, it's 68 yards and a touchdown to Ray Perkins. Perkins broke quickly, got behind Wilson, and Unitas, reaching down within for what makes the great ones great, got the ball to Perkins at the Oakland 35-yard line—50 yards in the air. From there, no one was close to Perkins.

SUPER BOWL V — PLAY #1

After Bulaich's last unsuccessful attempt at the Cowboys' front, Morrall calls a time-out and confers on the sideline with first-year head coach Don McCafferty and gets his play. McCafferty, with a call that makes you look like a genius if it works or a moron if it doesn't, elects to have Morrall go for the touchdown by passing to Mitchell in the corner of the end zone. Morrall waits for Mitchell to make his break and clear on the "corner" pattern, looks and throws in the direction of the second tight end. But it's just a little too long and Mitchell cannot get enough of it to bring it in. O'Brien's earlier miss of the point-after-touchdown not withstanding, those who give out such awards are preparing McCafferty's "goat horns" for not attempting the sure-thing (?) field goal.

SUPER BOWL V — PLAY #2

The play was brought in from Tom Landry and given to Craig Morton. It was a flare pass to Walt Garrison coming out of the left side of the Cowboy backfield. It was a relatively safe call, but Colt right cornerback, Jimmy Duncan, got a hand on the ball and tipped it over toward strong safety Rick Volk. The youngster out of the University of Michigan gathered it in and set out for the Cowboys' goal. He nearly made it. Only a desperation stop by Dallas wide receiver, Reggie Rucker saved the touchdown. Volk was nailed at the 3-yard line, but two "pops" by fullback Tom Nowatzke (the Colts' surprising leading ground-gainer in the game) got the long-awaited touchdown. O'Brien's point-after tied the score. While the results were disastrous, only an All-Pro Monday morning quarterback could seriously second-guess the Cowboy call.

SUPER BOWL V — PLAY #3

Jim O'Brien kicked and connected on the 3-pointer, something he was prepared to do, but there was a variance from the original script. The first-year man later told a reporter that he figured he would "get a shot at winning it, but in an overtime period." The timetable was moved up by Curtis' interception and return. Colt center, Bill Curry, made a true snap, Morrall provided a good "spot" and hold, and the kid named "Lassie," because of his long hair, made it good. It was inside the right upright by about 7 feet—the best kick of the day for O'Brien. After kicking, he came close to setting an Orange Bowl high-jump record. After returning to earth, he kicked off and watched Jerry Logan intercept a Morton's desperation pass, ending the game.

NFC PLAYOFF 1971 — PLAY #1

Brodie went with the screen pass, something he has thrown masterfully hundreds of times in his career. On this particular play, the results were disasterous. He faked to the right, turned quickly (perhaps too quickly) and threw left. He threw directly to a startled George Andrie, who admittedly was blocked out of the play. Andrie, a 6'7" giant of a defensive end, rumbled to the 2-yard line with his catch. Calvin Hill and the offense did the rest on two straight smacks at the line. It was Dallas 7 and San Francisco 0—enough to win.

AFC PLAYOFF 1971 — PLAY #1

Griese called play-action. He faked to Csonka going into the line, and this "froze" strong safety Rick Volk. Actually it not only froze him—he committed himself toward the line for a run, and Warfield sailed by him to take Griese's pass. Hauling it in around midfield, Warfield completed the 75-yard scoring play.

AFC PLAYOFF 1971 — PLAY #2

The give was to Nottingham off right tackle. He was caught by Miami's defense slanting the right way to stop the play and gained only 1 yard Miami took over on downs. Miami didn't get too far on the subsequent drive, but that fourth down would be as close as Baltimore would get the rest of the day.

SUPER BOWL VI — PLAY #1

With very little fanfare, head coach Tom Landry sent Mike Clark and the field-goal team onto the field. The well-traveled ex-Texas Aggie booted the ball through from 9 yards out and Dallas was on the board.

With very few exceptions, Super Bowl games have been panned as being dull and boring. Perhaps the football isn't of the thrill-a-minute variety, but there is good reason. An old NFL adage goes: offense sells tickets, defense wins championships. Putting some stock in that, a team that gets to the Super Bowl has to have an outstanding defensive unit. Thus, the teams lay back and wait for a mistake, no one being anxious to take the initiative. The 1971 version of the Dallas Cowboys fit the conservative/defensive mold. As it turned out, Clark's 3-pointer would have assured no less than a tie.

SUPER BOWL VI — PLAY #2

With a full half to play, although somewhat dominated by Dallas, Miami elected to go for the field goal. Yepremian got it through from 31 yards out. It got the Dolphins a score of some sort, and at the time that meant a great deal. Here was a young team in its Super Bowl versus a veteran team that had been in the Super Bowl before, not to mention many championship games. Although the Dolphins had not exactly frightened the Cowboys during the first half, they were still very much in the ball game at 10-3. Had Shula and his staff decided to go for the touchdown with a high-risk pass or some other method and come up with nothing, it would have been very hard to pump up the team for the second half. Again, the conservatism that seems to infect each Super Bowl was spreading to both sides of the field.

SUPER BOWL VI — PLAY #3

Taking a page from the "gadget section" of the Cowboys' thick and complicated play-book—something he'd do again in a future Super Bowl—Landy sent word in to run the flanker reverse with Hayes set to the left and coming back and running ight. The call worked very well. "Bullet Bob" bellied back deep, took the ball from Staubach and sped around right end as only he could. Traffic slowed Hayes down, and Miami defensive end Bob Heinz crossed the field and caught up with him—but not until Hayes had covered 16 yards down to the Miami 6-yard line. It was now first and goal at the 6, and the Cowboys seemed on the brink of breaking the game open. Two 3-yard punches at the Miami defense got the ball in the end zone—first by Garrison and then Thomas for the score, making it 17-3. There was more to come.

NFC PLAYOFF 1972 — PLAY #1

Billy Kilmer, whose throwing hand is very hot today (he'll complete 14 of 18 passes tried) elects to go deep. As suggested, Taylor ran the sideline with an "up" tacked on to it. The pass route begins just like the last one, looking as if Charley Taylor and Bill Kilmer will be content to get the catch for the first down. As Taylor nears the sideline, however, he plants his foot and cuts upfield. This leaves him free of Water's coverage and in a position to take Kilmer's toss. He does this and gets down to the Dallas 21-yard line before Waters recovers and makes the tackle. On the play, Kilmer's throw was a good 50 yards in the air. He wasn't supposed to have that kind of an arm. Later in this drive, Taylor will go inside on Waters. Waters won't be fooled, but he is helpless to stop a perfectly thrown ball, which will give the Skins another score.

AFC PLAYOFF 1972 — PLAY #1

Larry Seiple ran from punt formation—boy! did he run. Thirty-seven yards worth. This took him down to the Steelers' 12-yard line. If Seiple hadn't made it, Don Shula would not have been the man to "second-guess." It was Seiple himself who decided to run when he saw the Steelers made virtually no rush. "It wasn't in the play-book," Seiple would say later in the locker room. "I never thought of it until it opened up." Two plays later the score was tied as Csonka took a 9-yard swing pass in for the touchdown.

AFC PLAYOFF 1972 — PLAY #2

Griese wasted no time in showing that he came in to win, or at least go down giving it his best shot. Perhaps his best shot was this particular play—a look-in pass to Paul Warfield which netted 52 yards. Warfield was set wide to the left, but he angled sharply to the right and took Griese's throw. The man with the great speed, great hands, and fluid moves got the ball "underneath" the Steeler zone coverage and turned on the speed. He streaked to the Steeler 24-yard line before Mike Wagner angled over to stop him. Two plays later, Griese again went to Warfield, but a little more shallow this time. Jack Ham's interception showed what a great linebacker he is and pointed up Griese's still rusty arm. But Dwight White was ruled offside, and Miami got new life and a first down at the Pittsburgh 13-yard line.

AFC PLAYOFF 1972 — PLAY #3

Griese's call was Kiick over right tackle. Kiick not only got the yard, but tacked on another to the 2-yard line. He was stopped by Ernie Holmes, who supplements the Steeler front four of L. C. Greenwood, Joe Greene, Ben McGee, and Dwight White in goal-line situations. The next play was a repeat. Dolphins at right tackle, Steeler stop by Holmes. But on second down, Jim Kiick took a pitchout around right end, took cornerback John Rowser into the end zone with him, and took Miami into the lead.

SUPER BOWL VII — PLAY #1

Wanting to put some points up and make the most of the situation, Griese drops back and is waiting for Twilley to work his magic on Pat Fischer. This play presents one of the classic confrontations in all of pro football. Twilley, himself no giant at 5'10" and 185 pounds, is a "moves and hands" receiver rather than a speed-burner. Fischer, at 5'10" and 169 pounds, is a wily veteran of 12 years service. He's not blessed with much speed either, but he is very tough and extremely knowledgeable. On this particular play, however,

Twilley has turned Fischer completely around (the last thing a defensive back wants to allow), first by cutting inside and then by going outside. He takes Griese's pass at the 5-yard line and somehow manages to get a corner of the end zone as he and Fischer go sprawling over the goal-line marker.

SUPER BOWL VII — PLAY #2

Kilmer elected to come back with another pass. Although Kilmer had teamed up with Jerry Smith many times in similar situations with good success, he went to Charley Taylor, trying to find the seam in the Miami zone coverage. But super safety Jake Scott strengthened his claim on the game's Most Valuable Player award by taking the pass 3 yards deep in the end zone and returning it back down to the Washington 48-yard line. Only dogged pursuit by Charlie Harraway prevented a touchdown on the runback. Scott, in a postgame interview, made it sound all too easy. He said, "Lloyd and I (referring to Lloyd Mumphord) were covering Taylor, with Lloyd outside and me inside. Kilmer didn't see me cut over and the ball came to me." So did the ball game, the MVP award, and a lot of recognition.

SUPER BOWL VII — PLAY #3

Allen ignored all the free advice heaped his way and instructed Mike Bragg to use his regular method of kicking off. This Bragg did. Mercury Morris fielded the ball at the goal line and only got out to the 16-yard line (very good coverage, especially on the mercurial Morris). From there, the Dolphins got out to their 36-yard line before calling on Larry Seiple to punt out of danger on a fourth and 6 situation. Allen later would explain to newsmen that he felt there was too much time to try to execute the onside kick. He felt it was better to "kick deep, try to hold them, and hope to block the punt." His logic didn't work as Miami was not held—they even passed once for a first down—nor was the punt blocked, and on top of this, Washington was forced to call all of their time-outs while still on defense. Kilmer's offense got the ball back, but with only 1:14 left for a series of 4 passing plays that netted a −4 yards. The Dolphins took over as time ran out.

NFC PLAYOFF 1973 — PLAY #1

The call was Reed over the vacated left-guard hole. The Cowboys "filled" well, but Reed still got enough for the first down. But Minnesota was moved back with a penalty and a sack of Tarkenton, but Fred Cox salvaged the drive with a 44-yard field goal.

NFC PLAYOFF 1973 — PLAY #2

The give was to Chuck Foreman, as once again Viking coach Bud Grant took the calculated risk. Foreman got the inches and a couple of yards to spare. From the 11-yard line, Tarkenton scrambled for more yardage, and this was followed by Foreman sweeping right end for the touchdown.

NFC PLAYOFF 1973 — PLAY #3

Tarkenton called a deep pass to Gilliam, and like nearly everything else he did that day, it worked to perfection. Gilliam was wide open and made a 54-yard touchdown on the play. This gave the Vikings breathing room just when they needed it. They just added more "insurance" from there.

AFC PLAYOFF 1973 — PLAY #1

Oakland attempted the field goal. Blanda made it good from 21 yards out, but the 3 points were soon negated. Miami's return man, Charley Leigh, took the following kickoff back 52 yards and set up a 42-yard Garo Yepremian field goal.

SUPER BOWL VIII — PLAY #1

The play Griese called was a deep throw to Marlin Briscoe. The former league-leading pass-catcher got 13 of the 14 yards needed for the touchdown. Two cracks at the middle of the Viking line by Jim Kiick got the yard and the touchdown, the score coming behind center Jim Langer's block. This made the score 14-0, and the Vikings were really still in the starting blocks. This scoring drive also ate up a large chunk of time—to be exact, 5:46. The march was a ten-play affair, and quarterback Griese threw only twice. To show the consistent manner in which Miami gained ground, the pass to Briscoe was the longest play of the drive. Keep in mind that the first quarter has yet to expire.

SUPER BOWL VIII — PLAY #2

While the Viking running game isn't ripping huge, gaping holes in the Miami defense, Oscar Reed is running oftener, if not farther than any of the other Viking backs. He's big, and he's tough. Sensing a need for a touchdown, Bud Grant elects to go for the "3 inches." Much like the Philadelphia Eagles of the 1960s, who relied on All-Pro tackle Bob Brown's block to get back the daylight needed for crucial yardage, the Vikes put their trust in Yary to give Reed (or whichever back gets the call in a given situation) space to make the necessary distance. Whether or not Reed made the distance is immaterial. Nick Buoniconti met him in the hole and popped the ball loose for Jake Scott to recover. Seconds later, the half ends and Minnesota is still whitewashed.

SUPER BOWL VIII — PLAY #3

Bud Grant can't really afford to be less than wide open in his strategy for the upcoming kickoff. His Vikes make no attempt to disguise their intentions—he's loaded the kickoff team with as many quick "good-hands people" as he can. Miami was ready for the short kick, and they got it. Cox aimed his kick at combination linebacker-defensive end Bob Matheson, who was on the Miami front line. It hit him and rebounded, being recovered by the Vikings' Terry Brown, a defensive back. However, an overanxious "bomb-squadder," Ron Porter, a reserve linebacker, was ruled offside, and Minnesota had to kick over from 5 yards farther back. This dropped the probability of converting an onside kick down to about zero, and the Vikes kicked deep. The hepped-up Minnesota defense held Miami to 3, −2, and −15 yards on the ensuing series, but Seiple's 57-yard punt, downed by Mike Kolen at the Minnesota 3-yard line, all but shut the door on the Vikings.

NFC PLAYOFF 1974 — PLAY #1

Tark elected to throw deep and try for the touchdown. He got it. Jim Lash was free of Al Clark's coverage at the 1-yard line, and he took Tarkenton's pass. He simply stepped into the end zone for the first score of the game.

NFC PLAYOFF 1974 — PLAY #2

We don't know what Los Angeles was looking for, but what they got was Osborn off left guard. He leaped up and over, just barely getting into the end zone before being shoved back. The touchdown makes it 14-3, but there is still plenty of playing time left. Perhaps what influenced the Vikes to go for it was the fact that their drive took fifteen plays and close to 8 minutes to complete. This kept the ball away from the Rams a long time.

NFC PLAYOFF 1974 — PLAY #3

On a play that gets on magazine covers, as well as into highlight films, Harris hit little Harold Jackson crossing into the middle. The swifty took the pass without altering his stride at the 27-yard line. From there it was a sprint to the end zone, and Minnesota didn't have anyone to match Jackson's 9.5 speed.

AFC PLAYOFF 1974 — PLAY #1

Putting the earlier miss behind him, Gerela kicked the 23-yard field goal. Apparently at this juncture, head coach Chuck Noll felt it was important to get some points, having not done so on earlier opportunities. The field goal tied the game at 3-3 with most of the second quarter still to play. At this point, the Steelers were gaining confidence. The Oakland running game was nearly nonexistent, and Stabler was forced to throw more, but not with any great success. So far, the Oakland runners had only gained 15 yards on 8 attempts.

AFC PLAYOFF 1974 — PLAY #2

Bradshaw elected to go to Swann on a post pattern. The Steelers' number-one draft choice made a leaping catch (does he make any other kind?) for the touchdown that, for all intents and purposes, should have put the game away. But even though the Steel Curtain is dominating the game, Oakland isn't dead yeat—as we shall see.

AFC PLAYOFF 1974 — PLAY #3

Whether or not it was a feeling that the passing game was jelling isn't known, but the Raiders went for and got the 3 points on the Blanda field goal. In fact, it was the Steelers who got the "later" touchdown. Franco, on a second and 7, roared up the middle to score behind a wedge provided by center Ray Mansfield and guards Gerry Mullins and Jim Clack.

SUPER BOWL IX — PLAY #1

Breaking from tradition on first down, Tarkenton went for all the marbles with a pass. He sent John Gilliam curling deep into the middle of the Steeler secondary. Tark hit Gilliam at the 5-yard line. A 175-pound ground-to-air missile, disguised as Steeler free safety Glen Edwards, also hit Gilliam at the 5. The collision sent the ball into orbit, and as it returned toward earth, Mel Blount, super Steeler cornerback, picked it off at the goal line and returned it to the 10-yard line. Having checked the Viking offense, the Steelers were content to let the clock run out and take an 2-0 lead into the locker room. Although the Steelers had the slimmest of leads, their dominance of the game was beginning to show. Total offense for the first half read: Steelers 165 yards, Vikings 76 yards. More revealing were the passing stats. Terry Bradshaw was 5 for 9 and no interceptions. Tarkenton was forced to throw 18 times, completing only 7, and suffering the 1 critical interception.

SUPER BOWL IX — PLAY #2

Tarkenton varied from his set pattern and passed to his left, but it was deflated by Joe Greene this time. Not only did Greene tip the ball, but he brought it in for the interception and stomped 10 yards back upfield to the Steeler 45-yard line. To show just what Tarkenton was contending with all day, here was Joe Greene, a left defensive tackle, some 15 yards downfield on the defensive right side of the Pittsburgh set-up. The play illustrated the near-total frustration a Steeler opponent is confronted with. Even when Tarkenton and the Vikings went to sound, logical plays, the Steelers were there to thwart them. The Steelers didn't score after this break, but they did further demoralize the Vikes and at the same time consume valuable time.

SUPER BOWL IX — PLAY #3

Even though the Steelers' defense proved to be up to it later, Pittsburgh did not settle for a field goal. Disdaining field position and a field goal, Bradshaw rolled out to his right and saw Larry Brown—an underrated receiver, who had been a real clutch catcher in the Steelers' late season and playoff surge—was open. Bradshaw drilled the ball home, and Brown made the grab for a 4-yard touchdown. With Roy Gerela's extra point, the score read 16-6 in favor of Pittsburgh. Immediately after the kickoff, Tarkenton went deep to Gilliam in the middle. Mike Wagner, the Steelers' strong safety, got the pass and all but assured the win.

NFC PLAYOFF 1975 — PLAY #1

As if to amplify his statement that Harris is number one, Knox started him. He does little on the first series—no passes attempted. On the next series, he throws on second and 4, and it's intercepted by Dallas's D. D. Lewis. This sets up a Cowboy touchdown. Next he gets into a third and 8 situation, throws incomplete, and is replaced by Jaworski.

NFC PLAYOFF 1975 — PLAY #2

The Rams elected to go for a Dempsey 41-yard field-goal attempt. While Tom Henderson blocked the first try, this one got off cleanly, but it faded too much to the left and was no good. Getting the ball at the 24-yard line, Staubach put together a 9-play 76-yard drive to make it 14-0.

NFC PLAYOFF 1975 — PLAY #3

The call was to Preston Pearson on a pass into the end zone. While the call worked, 105 percent of the credit should go to Preston. He launched himself to making a diving, fingertip catch of the Staubach toss. The catch, one of the best of the season, made it 21-0. Pearson, incidentally, is the only Cowboy who is not "home grown." He was claimed on waivers from

Pittsburgh—all other Dallas players were draft choices or free agents originally signed by Dallas.

AFC PLAYOFF 1975 — PLAY #1

Bradshaw went deep to Stallworth. The second-year man, whose key block enabled Franco to score earlier, ran toward the back flag in the left corner of the end zone. Bradshaw's pass was right on target, and Stallworth made a fine leaping catch for the touchdown. Neal Colzie, a rookie starting the game for the injured Willie Brown, slipped on the bad turf on the play and later came in for a lot of criticism, but in all fairness, he wouldn't have had much position on Stallworth if he had stayed upright. Gerela couldn't convert, even though he tried a left-footed dropkick, necessitated by a bad snap; and the score remains Steelers 16 and Oakland 7.

AFC PLAYOFF 1975 — PLAY #2

The call was for a field goal. Blanda showed that there was still something left in his 48-year-old leg by pumping the 41-yard kick through. The call surprised some spectators and viewers, but there is nothing in the NFC Official Rule Book that says you have to get a touchdown first and then try for the field goal when you find yourself needing both. It was the kind of call that could win.

AFC PLAYOFF 1975 — PLAY #3

Stabler found Branch in front of Mel Blount at the 15-yard line. It was a 37-yard pass, but the clock ran out. Branch struggled to get out of bounds but couldn't. As is always the case in games like this, there were those who thought he may have gotten out before the clock ticked off its final seconds. It was not the case. A picture in a weekly sports magazine captured the moment beautifully. There is Branch struggling to drag Blount with him over the sidelines; he's still 10 yards in bounds, and the scoreboard clock shows :00 in the biggest, most final digits possible.

SUPER BOWL X — PLAY #1

As mentioned, all during the season the Steelers would only run from this formation. It was usually a handoff over the right side of the line, and Mullins would add his bulk and speed to the blocking by coming back toward the attack point. On this particular call, however, Bradshaw crossed up the Dallas defense by throwing. He spotted Grossman open at the goal line behind Dallas linebackers Lee Roy Jordan and Dave Edwards. Grossman made the catch and stepped in for the score. While Jordan and Edwards were closest to Grossman, this is not to say that he was the responsibility of either of them. Often a hustling defender tries to compensate for a teammate only to find himself in the position of looking "stung." Seconds later, Roy Gerela's extra point made the score even at 7-7.

SUPER BOWL X — PLAY #2

Perhaps the Steelers really wanted to get the upper hand in their showdown battle with Dallas, since they did elect to go on "fourth and short." The strategy was good, but the play wasn't. Bradshaw passed out into the right flat toward Franco. The big running back got his hands on the ball, but so did Dallas's leading "hitter," Cliff Harris. Cliff flew into Franco with considerable force, and the ball fell harmlessly to the turf. Dallas then took over on downs, but a Roger Staubach third-and-1 pass to Robert Newhouse, whom the Steelers came close to drafting in 1972 in lieu of Franco, was overthrown. Mitch Hoopes punted away on fourth down. The score remained at 10-7, Dallas, as the first half ended. While Pittsburgh's gamble could hardly be included in "The Best Plays of the Year," the spectators were excited to see two teams attempting to break out of the conservative mold.

SUPER BOWL X — PLAY #3

Steeler head coach Chuck Noll surprised nearly everyone in the Orange Bowl, including some of his own players, by not punting. Instead, he called the punting team back and left the offensive unit on the field with instructions to run on fourth down. Later, Noll was to tell the press that the play was not necessarily selected with the thought of gaining a first down. Hanratty handed off to Bleier off right tackle. He got 2 yards before being downed by Ed "Too Tall" Jones. It was the Cowboys' ball now at their own 34-yard line. Staubach got to midfield on a keeper and a razzle-dazzle play to Preston Pearson got down to the Steeler 33-yard line; but from there it was just three "hope and pray" passes, the last of which was picked off by Glen Edwards and returned 30 yards as time ran out. Noll would later explain that the Steelers relied on their "Steel Curtain" defense all season long, "So why change now?"